# HOW TO BECOME A
# WORKING ACTOR

# HOW TO BECOME A
# WORKING ACTOR

## Susan Wright

A Citadel Press Book
*Published by Carol Publishing Group*

A Citadel Press Book
Published by Carol Publishing Group
Citadel Press is a registered trademark of Carol Communications, Inc.

Editorial, sales and distribution, rights and permissions inquiries should be addressed to
Carol Publishing Group, 120 Enterprise Avenue, Secaucus, N.J. 07094

In Canada: Canadian Manda Group, One Atlantic Avenue, Suite 105, Toronto, Ontario
M6K 3E7

Carol Publishing Group books may be purchased in bulk at special discounts for sales
promotion, fund-raising, or educational purposes. Special editions can be created to
specifications. For details, contact Special Sales Department, Carol Publishing Group,
120 Enterprise Avenue, Secaucus, N.J. 07094.

Manufactured in the United States of America

10  9  8  7  6  5  4  3  2  1

Library of Congress Cataloging-in-Publication Data

Wright, Susan (Susan G.)
    How to become a working actor / Susan Wright.
        p.   cm.
    ISBN 0–8065–1881–2 (pbk.)
    1. Acting—Vocational guidance.   I. Title.
PN2055.W75   1997
792'.028'023—dc21                          97–4066
                                              CIP

In Memory of Barry Douglas

# Contents

# *Introduction*

**Tina Johnson**

People tend to think of show business rather like they think of the lottery: if you possess that rare, winning combination, you just might make a fortune. Young actors often rely on that luck, hoping to be at the right place at the right time. But do you really want to depend on winning the lottery to make a living?

The truth is that becoming a working actor takes an incredible amount of skill and accumulated experience and incurs a lot of heartbreak along the way. The only way to become a working actor is to treat it like you would any other business. All the training and skill in the world won't do you any good if you don't know where to go to get the type of work you want or how to pursue the professionals in order to land auditions and roles.

The key to this book is the word "working." There are plenty of brilliant coaches and experienced actors out there who can help you acquire training and develop technique. This book, however, is a practical guide, intended to give you the nuts-and-bolts business knowledge you need to survive, and even thrive, as an actor. It will show you how to conquer the system, covering everything from photographs and resumés to auditions to casting directors. It will tell you where to go to find the acting jobs you want and how to get them once you've found them.

These are the basics of the business. I know because I've

made my living as an actor for most of my life, for more than twenty years now. On Broadway, I've appeared in *Damn Yankees, She Loves Me, Best Little Whorehouse in Texas, Festival,* and *South Pacific.* I've been in the national and Broadway versions of *State Fair,* and worked in Off-Broadway, stock, and regional productions. I also lived and worked for four years in LA, where I guest-starred on *Empty Nest, Newhart,* and *Murphy Brown* and had long running parts in the soaps *Texas* and *Search for Tomorrow.*

I'm like most of the people who work in this business. We're the actors you never know about—the chorus in a Broadway play or the character actors or guest stars on TV, the people that fill in around the leads. We're the actors who make our living in show business.

Choosing an acting career can be a rewarding experience if you love acting. But you have to love acting above everything else to be successful because only then can you withstand the heartbreak. When you lose a role you really wanted or mess up an audition, you have to give yourself time to be upset, then learn to put it behind you as soon as possible so you can face the next challenge. You have to be tough enough not to take rejection personally; otherwise, if there's anything else you might be interested in doing, you should do it.

You have to know yourself, and I know I'm not happy unless I'm acting. The times when I've struggled the most were the times when I lost my self-esteem or my focus. You have to be able to deal with the self-doubt and worry when you're not working, and to stop thinking "That's the last job I'll ever get!" I learned that you have to make your own challenges, so even when I'm not working I still make my schedule for the week around acting; taking classes, doing aerobics, and seeing shows.

Many people are drawn to an acting career because they want to be the star—the leading lady or man, the one in the spotlight. But that isn't what acting is about. Finding out who you are as an actor, discovering the roles that suit you, and the type of acting you do best takes time. I've found that I'm more comfortable when I have a very strong emotional reaction to a character. But I didn't learn that from college training.

It pays to listen to advice from the professionals in the business. It was a class at HP Studios in New York that first gave me a realistic picture of myself. Aaron Frankel taught me most about who I was from the material he gave me and the roles he chose for me. I was able to rely on him and feel secure in my ability to perform, and this in turn gave me a chance to focus.

One of my acting teachers, Michael Howard, told me that you have to use what God gave you. You're not going to change that. I remember at one point a casting director actually said to my agent, "You know Tina is a wonderful actress, but she'll never do Shakespeare." I never performed Shakespeare except in college (and that doesn't count), but then, naturally, I wanted to do it. "Wait a minute," I said, "I *can* do Shakespeare!" But that casting director was right; that's not the way my career has gone.

You have to rely on your own instincts. Many people keep telling me that I should be on a sitcom. I was even advised to do a comedy act so I could get a TV series, but I resisted that because I trained as an actor, not as a stand-up comedian. I'm a good actor, and I can be funny, and those are the roles that tend to suit me. I'll just have to land them without going the comedy club route.

My agents have been my best guides during my career. I've been lucky to have very good agents, both theatrical and commercial, and in this book you'll get good advice on finding your own agent. You have to watch out for people who just try to make money off actors, especially if you're younger, without considering what's most important for your career in the long run. It takes a good agent to aim your career toward longevity.

For example, I played Angel in *Best Little Whorehouse in Texas*, as southern a role as you could get. Then I portrayed Lurlene Harper in *Texas*, and went from that into Rhonda Sue, a ditzy Southern girl, on *Search for Tomorrow*.

It was time for me to shift. We had some other offers for

Southern roles at that point and turned them down. I didn't want to get stereotyped, which was the right decision for me since I've done some really interesting work that I wouldn't have gotten otherwise, like a British character in *Christina Albert's Father* by Polly Pen (based on the book by Victor Herbert). It's also come full circle—people still remember me for my earlier Southern roles and still call me for parts reminiscent of my earlier work.

I worked constantly in theater for my first eight years in New York. Those were incredible years, which made it even more difficult for me when the tough times came. It had never occurred to me that I could be out of work. So when it happened, and it happened for a couple of years when I was in my thirties, it was difficult for me. Aging for women in this business is awful *unless* you can continue to create some of your own work. Our culture is focused on youth and "beauty" but I admire women like Katharine Hepburn and Anjelica Huston who are unconventional and very successful. You have to look to your own beauty, not what the business wants to impose on you. That thirties niche is hard because you're no longer an ingenue, you're not a character actor, and you are not a leading lady.

It was an awful time in my life. I had been on Broadway, and now I was waitressing again. Once a customer told me he remembered me from *Best Little Whorehouse in Texas*. He asked, "So what—did you quit acting?" I replied, "No, but I like to eat." People who aren't in this business don't understand the difficulties. They think it's wonderful when they hear you're working on Broadway, but they don't see the downside.

It was during this period that I went to Los Angeles. In some ways show business on the West Coast is a totally different business. But I stuck to what I knew best—the theatrical side of the business. I worked through theatrical agents even though Los Angeles is more television oriented. And it worked. I got television roles because of my theatrical work. The director of *Murphy Brown* knew me from New York and cast me in a guest-star role. I was also cast in my first long-running soap from a

Broadway play; I got cast for the second soap from the first.

It takes perseverance to be a working actor. Lots of actors drop out because they get tired of the job-to-job lifestyle. I like acting, but I don't really like the acting lifestyle, not knowing where my next dime is coming from. But most dedicated career actors learn for themselves (usually between acting jobs) that they aren't suited to a 9–5 job. There's something inside us that needs a less structured lifestyle.

You also have to be financially smart to make it through the slow times. When I got a role in my first soap opera, *Texas*, I invested in an apartment in New York. It's put pressure on me to make a lot of money, but now not only do I have my career, I have something to show for it.

Many people don't realize you don't have to live in New York or Los Angeles to work steadily as an actor. I have a friend who was in six Broadway shows, but when he got married he didn't want to raise a child in New York. So he and his wife moved to Florida, and he's doing very well down there. He's still acting and he's happy.

Regional theater is a wonderful opportunity for an actor. You can take risks and do work that wouldn't be produced in New York. And you're free of the New York critics. People get scared in New York because there's so much riding on each audition and every performance.

For example, *State Fair* received brilliant reviews all over the country but when the play made it to New York, the critics killed it. A few people had the power to close the show. And that show was good. It was a corny, old-fashioned Rodgers and Hammerstein musical, and every theatrical person I knew, the people I thought would put it down, loved it. Barry Moss, a New York casting director, saw it five times. I even recently had an audition because the casting director saw me in *State Fair*, and he loved the show. But that's the business.

In an actor's life there is no turning point where your career gels for good. Success takes work; a career is a process. You have to keep yourself together and take it one step at a time. I still allow myself my moments of grief and anguish, like when I give the best audition of my life and I don't even get a callback. You just have to keep auditioning and doing the best you can do that day. I often console myself by thinking there's a reason I didn't get a particular part and that I'm going to wait around to see what that reason is. Maybe I'm meant to learn something from the experience. Maybe another, better opportunity will come along that would never have come if I'd gotten the first part. So I get up the next morning and I go to aerobics or I go to my dance class. I keep making my own challenges every day.

Good work doesn't go unnoticed. If you hang in there and are committed to your work, then you will be remembered. People are watching. I met both Rob Marshall and Randy Skinner three and four years, respectively, before I worked with them. Rob remembered me from an audition in LA when he was casting for *She Loves Me on Broadway* and Randy remembered me from an audition in New York and cast me in *Pal Joey* in LA.

As I get older I find I'm mainly auditioning for people I know. The casting directors call for me; they know my work. I've built a career as an actor, and I have plenty to show for it.

If I could start over again, I'd do it all over. The most important thing is to love what you do and to love the people you are surrounded by. If what you truly love is acting, in any way and every chance you get, then you can become a working actor.

—Tina Johnson

# HOW TO BECOME A
# WORKING ACTOR

# 1 | *The Basics of the Acting Profession*

Actors mainly find work in theater, film, television, commercials, and industrials. The theater can encompass any sort of live performance including musicals, whether the actor is performing on Broadway in New York City or on a cruise ship in the Caribbean. Film usually refers to a feature-length production, whether it is intended for television or movie screen. Television work ranges from daily soaps to prime-time, while commercial work refers to any sort of product advertisement, whether it's a ten second local spot or an hour-long infommercial. Industrials are usually some type of employee training film, and include dramatizations, demonstrations, and voice-overs.

Each of these media require vastly different things from actors—technically, stylistically, and logistically. Many people think you have to live in New York to be a working actor in the theater, but in reality Chicago is considered to be better for young actors who want to work on the stage. And while Los Angeles is where most television is cast, New York also has a large number of studios. In fact, almost every city has gotten its shot at a prime-time series, bringing in plenty of work for local actors (*Dallas, Miami Vice,* and *Northern Exposure,* to name a few).

For steady work, many actors turn to commercials and industrials. There's a vast amount of acting work available in the corporate sector, including live shows, safety/training

3

movies, and sales videos. There are also regional and dinner theaters in most major cities.

Actors often seek several types of work in order to make an adequate living. Chapter 7 of this guide will tell you what type of work is readily available in your area.

But how do you find work? Ask a working actor, and they'll always say it's the people you know, the people who see you act and remember you, who hire you for that next job. It's all networking. If you're just starting out, ask your teacher to write an introduction for you to any agents or casting directors that they know. Follow up every lead, even if you already have an agent—it's up to you to drive your own career. This means you have to know the acting business and be informed about what's going on.

Following are a few of the basics of the acting profession, such as industry guides and trade papers, and venues where an actor can be seen. The guides listed in this book are the recognized publications in the industry. Any other guide that promises to give you the "inside scoop" on influential producers and executives is probably puffed up with nothing more than gossip.

The same goes for telecast services who promise to promote you over cable channels. Even if your tape does get on the air, it's playing while casting directors are busy at work. Professionals don't sit at home watching their cable channels on television to find talent.

## Advertisements

Even reputable publications such as *Back Stage* and *Drama Logue* don't screen their advertisements. Avoid ads calling for "new faces" and "experience unnecessary." In this business, experience is almost always necessary.

Also watch out for companies offering photo and resumé counseling. By following the tips in this book, and by choosing a good photographer and image consultant, you can do far more for yourself than they can.

In general, any talent agency, acting school, or modeling/ acting ad that runs every day in the newspaper is probably raking in cash from actors, not producers.

### Industry Guides

The annual directories for stage, screen, and television include listings for actors and are regularly used by casting personnel. Only actors who belong to the unions (SAG and AFTRA, see chapter 3) can be listed in the *Academy Players Directory*. It's one of the major benefits of joining the union, so make sure you send them a recent, excellent photo!

*Academy Players Directories*
ADDRESS: 8949 Wilshire Blvd., 4th Floor, Beverly Hills, CA 90211

This guide is published three times a year by the Academy of Motion Picture Arts and Sciences. Listings are divided into four categories: leading men and juveniles, leading ladies and ingenues, character men and boys, character women and girls. Entries include name, photo, agent, and contact number. Listings are $20 per release.

### Trade Papers

Along with local trade papers that are listed in chapter 7, you can consult the nationwide trades to keep abreast of current productions. Some actors say they've never read the trades, while others rely on them for their coverage of the different types of acting work available.

For the East Coast, *Back Stage: The Performing Arts Weekly* has been the primary source of casting information for New York actors and regional theater for over thirty years. *Back Stage West* is the Los Angeles version, yet many actors claim that *Drama Logue* is the best trade publication for finding work on the West Coast.

*Variety* provides a broader picture of the acting industry in its weekly publication, and is perhaps the most famous trade.

The daily publications are *Hollywood Variety* and *The Hollywood Reporter*. These offer inside information on movie and television, including gossip and rumors about the deals and doings of production executives, actors, and agents. Though they aren't of much use for finding a job, they can give you an idea of industry trends and the general preferences of casting directors and directors. These dailies are readily available at newsstands in most major metropolitan cities.

*Back Stage*
ADDRESS: 1515 Broadway, 14th Floor, New York, NY 10036
This publication provides the best casting information for New York actors working in movie, television, or on the stage. It provides monthly lists of upcoming movies and plays along with the detailed information that an actor needs, including production staff, storyline and characters, stars' roles that have been signed, and most importantly, contact information for the casting director.

Actors who are looking for work in regional theater can also find numerous listings of productions (both union and nonunion work), along with contact information. One issue a year is devoted to special topics: off-Broadway theaters, regional theaters and how to audition for them, dinner theaters, cabaret opportunities, theme parks, outdoor festivals, and cruise ships.

*Backstage* features columns by professionals in the industry such as directors, writers, directors, and choreographers, with advice for performers on auditioning and technique. There are also regular commentaries on union matters and the legal wrangles within the industry, particularly about those things that can directly affect you as a working actor.

*Drama Logue*
PHONE: (213) 464–5079
ADDRESS: P.O. Box 38771, Los Angeles, CA 90038
This publication is mainly geared for actors on the west coast, and includes numerous casting notices for theater,

movie, television, and cabaret. It also provides in-depth interviews with casting directors, actors, producers, and directors, as well as advertising for schools, resources, professional photographers, and private coaches.

*Ross Reports Television*
PHONE: (718) 937–3990
ADDRESS: 40-29 27th St, Long Island City, NY 11101

This monthly booklet is geared toward actors looking for work in television, with listings of productions and casting information for the daytime serials, prime-time network shows, and television variety productions such as Saturday Night Live. For actors looking for commercial work, this booklet contains listings of commercial packagers, advertising agencies, and talent agencies. Each listing contains valuable information on whether they accept pictures and resumés, videotape or audiotapes, and the best way for an actor to approach them for work.

*Theatrical Index*
PHONE: (212) 951–8800
ADDRESS: Price Berkeley, 888 Eighth Ave, New York, NY 10019

This weekly booklet lists current plays in production in New York, both on Broadway and off-Broadway. It includes a capsule summary of the play and descriptions of available roles, as well as the name of the casting director, producer, playwright, and director.

*Variety*
ADDRESS: 475 Park Avenue South, New York, NY 10016

This publication is available every Wednesday and includes news about the business aspects of the performing arts such as movie grosses, television deals, and record contracts. A limited amount of space is devoted to casting news.

*Breakdown Services*
PHONE: (310) 276–9166

ADDRESS: 1120 South Robertson, 3rd Floor, Los Angeles CA 90035

Agents used to have to go to the studios and read the scripts themselves to "break them down" and figure out which of their clients were suited to the roles. Then twenty-five years ago, Gary Marsh formed his company after he started breaking down scripts for his mother who was an agent.

Agents usually get breakdowns from Breakdown Services every day in order to stay on top of casting in theater, television, movie, and commercial productions. If you don't have an agent, subscribing to Breakdown Services is the best way to find out about suitable roles. That way you can strategically send your photo and resumé (P&R) to casting directors specifying a role in their current production.

Breakdowns consist of descriptions of the roles and characters that are needed, as well as other information such as the dates of the production and the names of the director and creative staff. The role descriptions are usually written by the head writer, so careful attention should be paid to the wording. Is the woman described as "fresh and lovely" or "fresh and spunky"? The desired interpretation of the role can be quite different based on a single adjective.

Breakdown Services is based in California, but it supplies information for the entire industry. You can get a year's subscription for only $41.30. Breakdown Services even provides pre-addressed mailing labels (at a small additional cost) for casting directors and agents on both coasts so you can do a mass mailing. Yet keep in mind that a personalized cover letter targeting a specific role will have the most impact.

### Other Publications

*Variety* and the daily Hollywood trade papers are not the only way to get up-to-the minute news about the industry. To find out about agencies, production companies, and the hot deals, there are also weeklies such as *Advertising Age*, *Ad-*

*Week, Broadcasting, CableVision,* and *Shoot!*

As for theater, *American Theater* is a monthly magazine that surveys stage productions throughout the country. It often prints the entire script of a new play. *Soap Opera Digest* is written for fans, but it is extremely useful for actors auditioning for daytime TV because of the character condensations and plot summaries of each show.

There are also publications that are geared more toward a general audience, but include gossip and articles that can offer insights for the beginning actor such as *Theater Week, Premiere,* and *Entertainment Weekly.*

### Talent Books

Talent books are compilations of pictures and resumés that are distributed to casting and industry personnel, while talent banks sometimes include audio and video cassettes. These compilations are made available to casting and industry personnel in the local area.

Actors must either belong to the sponsoring organization or pay to be included in talent books and banks. (For more specific information in your area, see chapter 7.)

### Talent Showcases

Showcases are forums in which actors perform scenes, songs, and monologues for directors and casting agents. They are often theatrical productions, with one or more actors performing several scenes in a row.

Several professional showcases take place throughout the country primarily for summer stock theater, while many others are organized on a local level by acting schools and actors' associations. (For more specific information in your area, see chapter 7.)

### Open Calls

Open calls are auditions that are held by casting personnel, producers, and directors. Any actor may come and sign up for an audition slot. Usually open calls are held for two reasons: when people are needed for atmosphere (like an open call for punk rockers), or when a specific, hard-to-cast role needs to be filled.

Announcements for open calls appear in the trade publications and usually they are quite specific about what type of actor is needed and what must be done for the audition.

Hundreds of amateurs tend to show up at open calls, so make sure you have a professional P&R and are suited to the part. And be prepared or all you'll do is make a bad impression on the casting personnel who are there.

## Talent Search

Talent searches are conducted by the casting personnel of daytime soap operas when they are looking for a fresh pool of actors to gives the soap a more real, diverse atmosphere. Once a talent search has been announced, actors can submit their P&Rs through their agents or independently if they don't have representation. Actors will be chosen for auditions on the basis of their P&R.

## Eligible Performer Auditions (EPAs)

The unions require producers to set aside time for open casting in which all members of the union are eligible for an audition slot. There is no limit to the number of people who may sign up, but only the first 115 are guaranteed to be seen per day. There is also no carryover to the next day, so be sure to get there early on the first day to get a prime slot.

These EPAs must be held before any other auditions and before any cast members (other than the stars) have been signed. Yet the unfortunate fact is some of the roles have already been tentatively assigned by the casting director and they are just going through the formality of the EPA.

## The LORT Lottery

Regional theaters provide a five-day EPA two times a year. Casting personnel of the League of Regional Theaters (LORT) travel to New York, Chicago, or Los Angeles where they screen 400 actors in each region for the first three days. The second two are spent auditioning selected performers who get four minutes each to perform their monologues. You can participate in LORT by mailing in a request for an audition.

Usually there are specific roles that need to be filled in various productions, but even if you don't suit the available parts or meet the producers' immediate needs, your audition can have impact on the casting personnel. Keep in touch with photo-postcards, and perhaps next year when casting begins for new productions, you will be considered.

# 2 | *P&R*

P&R stands for photograph and resumé. A professional, compelling P&R is essential to your success as an actor. Here are some tips on making sure that your P&R are the best they can be.

## Your Photograph

Your picture, also called your head shot, is the first and often the last chance you have to make an impression on talent agents and casting directors. But it's very important not to make the mistake of using your photograph to glamorize yourself. The picture should look like *you*, the person who shows up for the audition. If you and the picture don't match, you'll never be seen by the people who could use you—and the ones who do call you won't be able to use you.

The quality of your photograph should be superior. This is one place no expense should be spared. And you should regularly make new photos to hand out to casting personnel. Perhaps there's an angle or type of lighting that's magic for your face; you just won't know it until people start to respond.

Make sure that the focus of the shot is on *you*. Don't allow fussy backgrounds or contrasting colors in clothing to distract from your face. Avoid jewelry, printed materials, and dramatic hairstyles. After all, your face is your calling card.

Single black and white headshots are usually preferred by

actors working in theater, movies, television, and industrials. Yet some actors prefer photographs that show them from the waist up because it enables them to convey more of their personal style or unique physique. Other actors say that limits you to certain roles.

Composite photographs are used to show different aspects of an actor and are preferred by character actors and actors who work in commercials. Several different photographs are grouped on one 8 x 10 sheet, showing various poses and outfits. Consult with your agent before you decide to put together a composite.

### Photographer

Find the *best* photographer you can—and if you are a regional actor it's worth it to travel to New York, Chicago, or LA to make sure you have quality shots. Not only do professional photographers understand the business and what it takes to create an appropriate and attention-getting photograph, but they are also great sources of information about the business.

The cost of a photo session can range from $125 to $650. You'll find many photographers listed in the trade publications, but don't stop there. Before laying out money for a photographer, network among the local actors. Which photographers are used most often by the top actors?

Next, make appointments to take a serious look at the portfolios of the photographers recommended to you. Visit at least three people before choosing one. In addition to inspecting the quality of their work, you will want to talk to each photographer to see who you feel most comfortable with. It's important to find someone who will know how to work with you to bring out your best qualities.

Inquire about the length of the photography session. You won't want to be rushed for this vital component of your career. Find out how many shots will be taken and how much each print will cost.

Many of the best photographers have experienced hair and makeup artists on staff who can prepare you for your shoot. You should discuss the backgrounds and color choice of your clothes with the photographer prior to the shoot. Photographers can sometimes shoot you in more than one way, providing many options for your final selection. But always remember that the photographer is working for you, and that you have to maintain control over what gets done and how.

### Your Appearance

The photograph should appear natural, a true reflection of yourself. Ask a casting director the qualities he or she looks for in an actor and the word you hear most often, for most roles, is "real." They all hate to call in an actor only to find that the person who walks through the door barely resembles the photograph they saw.

In many ways, an actor's photograph is an indicator of their professionalism. Only when you are confident with exactly who you are and what you look like will you be able to make an impact on people in the industry. Choosing a photograph that makes you look thinner or diminishes your large nose is self-defeating. Casting directors want actors who are unique, and they seek out interesting features in every photograph they see. Give them something to notice.

One well-known casting director tells actors to choose a photograph that your mother would love. It may not be your favorite, but casting directors will certainly know how to appreciate it.

An open and accessible facial expression will always win you interviews, while a sultry or brooding look usually backfires. And don't use affected poses with your hand on your chin or cheek.

Your smile should look relaxed and friendly. But keep in mind that the key to a good photograph is in the eyes—they should draw in the viewer, radiating confidence. Look straight at the camera, and be right there.

The best way to practice for your photo shoot is to have a friend take photos of you with a Polaroid. Take your time and be natural. Only by studying your face in all its natural expressiveness can you discover the best looks and angles for you.

Needless to say, you can also find out what angles minimize double chins, wrinkles, squinting, bags under your eyes, and prominent gums. A good photographer can also sparingly touch up your image without making you look unnatural. For character actors, exaggerated features are an asset.

The goal is to look attractively natural, not perfect. However there is some unspoken, absolute rule that actors must have good teeth. Most working actors have some, if not all, of their teeth capped. If you are just starting out and your teeth are noticeably uneven, you can get temporary fillers from your dentist.

Your clothes and hair will help establish your style. Bring a few different outfits, as well as pieces that can be layered for different effects: vests, silk shirts, tanks tops, jackets. Are you trying to work in industrials? Then wear a suit. Commercials? Then casual clothing is best. And if you've chosen to create a composite, bring distinctive clothing types such as yuppie mom, corporate executive, and outdoorsy thirtysomething.

It's a good idea to get the advice of an experienced image consultant. That way you'll find out what hairstyles, necklines, and colors suit you the best. You can also get tips on makeup, eyebrow shape, type of earrings to wear, and much more.

Make sure your hair is colored and styled before the shoot. Dark hair can disappear without well-placed highlights, while unruly bangs or curls can overpower your face. Find a stylist who works with theatrical clientele and who understands that what you require is far different from the kind of primping wedding participants and prom queens need.

### Contact Sheets

About a week after your shoot, your photographer will give you a set of contact sheets. These are pages of all the prints that were taken. Use a magnifying glass to see exactly what the photos look like.

Pick out at least half a dozen that you like and write the frame numbers on the back of the sheets. Then ask other people for their opinions. By all means, get the opinion of your friends and lovers, but don't rely on them for objective choices. It's best to find out what other actors think, and definitely consult your agent if you have one. And if you are lucky enough to be friendly with someone in casting, by all means show him or her the contact sheets and listen to his or her opinion. That's the audience you're aiming for, so why not go straight to the top?

You can chose several shots and have several photographs made depending on the role you want. Many actors also create photo-postcards they can mail to casting personnel and directors, reminding them of your experience or notifying them of upcoming appearances.

There's also a rage in the industry for photo-business cards. These have a postage-stamp-size photo on a business card, along with your name and contact number, and are easier to carry around than postcards or 8 x 10s for those impromptu moments when you're networking or just out socializing and happen meet people in the business. It's quite natural to hand someone your business card the first time you meet.

You don't have to use the same photo for the different formats. In fact, it's better to be able to give casting personnel your 8 x 10, then follow up with a different shot on postcards keeping them updated on your current work. And certain poses and expressions work better than others for the small size of the photo on the business card.

### *Duplication*

When you have chosen the shots you want to use, you can take the photographer's finished prints (lightly touched up to present the best you) to a duplicating service. The photographer will usually be able to recommend a reliable place.

Have the photo you've chosen for your headshot framed by a white border, and pay the extra amount required to have your name and telephone number printed on the front. Resumés often get separated from photos, and this will ensure that your name and face are indelibly linked together.

Order several hundred 8 x 10 copies at once. You'll need them, and bulk orders save you money. Most actors choose semi-matte paper for their prints since it doesn't show smudges like glossy paper does, yet has more light and life than matte paper.

Also order a few hundred photo-postcards. These are printed on cardstock, like a typical postcard. To mail them, you can either just stamp and address the back, or put it in an envelope to protect the picture from postmarks.

## Your Resumé

Whatever you do, don't lie on your resumé. Casting personnel know the industry far, far better than you, and your lie will inevitably be discovered. Casting directors like to exchange stories about actors they've caught, sometimes quite unintentionally, while conversing about their experience. In fact, there are plenty of stories of actors submitting their falsified resumé to the very person who cast the production the actor lied about being in!

Even if you have very little experience, your resumé can highlight your education, special skills, and training. Training can be a huge asset, particularly when you've taken classes with respected coaches.

Staple the resumé to the back of your picture—print side out—then trim the excess paper down to the size of the 8 x 10 photo. Don't print information on the back of the photo because as you work you will want to quickly update your resumé to showcase your recent experience. Besides, it seems amaturish, as does arriving at an audition with your resumé and photograph not yet stapled together.

Most casting directors prefer that the resumé be printed on white paper rather than tricky, eye-catching colors such as green or vibrant yellow. These can create an impression that goes counter to the type of character they are looking for. The same goes for pastel shades, though to a lesser degree.

Your resumé should be typed or typeset in a clear, easy-to-read format. Another useful marketing trick is to include a 2 x 3 picture on your resumé, in the upper right-hand corner for example. This way you can provide another type of pose or look, and your picture is still with your resumé even if the sheets become separated.

### Format

In the center at the top of the page, put your name, phone number (indicate whether it's a service or a machine), and union affiliation. If you are in the union, put your social security number underneath since it is important for clearing necessary paperwork.

If you have an agent, include his or her name and number as your contact. Never put your own address on the resumé because you'll be distributing it to hundreds of people, and you never know who might get hold of it. If you don't have an agent, you can get a mailbox at the post office.

At the top of your resumé, you should list your vital statistics: height, weight, and hair and eye color. This is the first place casting directors look.

Experience is listed by type of work you've done rather than chronologically. In New York the order is usually theater, television, movie, industrials, and commercials, while in Los Angeles it's movie, television, theater, industrials, and commercials.

Your credits should include the name of the production, your role, and the company who produced it. If you've done work in movies, then list the director as well as the company. With commercials, don't list your credits one by one; just state whether you have tape or voice-overs available. You don't want to miss out on auditions because you've already done two car commercials and the advertising executive doesn't want to risk customers having seen you on the air representing the competitor. Noncompete clauses last different lengths of time depending on where and for how long the commercial is aired. When you have signed a noncompete clause for a commercial that's on the air, then don't waste the casting personnel's time by auditioning for similar products.

At the end of your resumé, list your training and education, including the names of coaches, acting schools, and colleges. This is particularly important for actors who have less experience—casting personnel are often familiar with the teachers at acting schools and major universities. Casting directors also respect an actor who has spent years learning his or her craft, so include any actors' workshops or improvisational groups you've been involved with.

One sure way to catch a casting director's attention is to include special skills that you have. Any physical or language skills can be of potential use, such as racket sports, gymnastics, scuba diving, and rollerblading; ballroom, jazz, and tap dancing; or French, Spanish, or American Sign Language. But make sure you are proficient at the skills. If you get a part requiring them, you'll be asked to perform them over and over again in order to get the right shot.

Under special skills you can also include distinctive or unusual experiences you've had—modeling in another country, working in the Peace Corps, or training as a professional race car driver for example. After looking at a hundred resumés a week, a casting director will appreciate seeing anything thought-provoking.

## Videotape

If you have some professional footage of yourself, you can create a videotape that will do more to impress agents and casting personnel than your P&R would. Always get a copy of the work you do, whether it's a test for a soap opera for NBC or an under-five (a part consisting of five lines or less)in a local PBS drama.

The *composite* reel combines the speaking roles you've done to best advantage. You can tape any performances that appear on television, and take those along with copies of commercials and movie clips to an editing studio. They will create a 3/4" professional-quality tape for you, which can be copied without loss of image onto standard 1/2" VCR tapes. Don't try to make a tape-to-tape copy on your own—the quality will degrade to the point that the tape will look amateurish.

# TINA JOHNSON
## SAG * AFTRA * AEA

**COMMERCIALS:**
SEMM-627-5500

**TELEVISION**

| | | |
|---|---|---|
| EMPTY NEXT | Guest Star | Steve Zuckerman |
| NEWHART | Guest Star | Michael Lessac |
| MURPHY BROWN | Guest Star | Barnet Kelman |
| TEXAS | Lurlene Harper | |
| SEARCH FOR TOMORROW | Rhonda Sue | |

**BROADWAY**

| | | |
|---|---|---|
| STATE FAIR | Vivian/Ensemble | James Hammerstein/Randy Skinner |
| DAMN YANKEES | Ensemble | Jack O'Brien |
| SHE LOVES ME | Ensemble | Scott Ellis |
| BEST LITTLE WHOREHOUSE IN TEXAS | Angel | Pete Masterson/Tommy Tune |
| FESTIVAL | Shepherdess | Wayne Bryan |
| SOUTH PACIFIC | Ensemble | New York City Opera |

**NATIONAL TOUR**

| | | |
|---|---|---|
| STATE FAIR | Ensemble | James Hammerstein/Randy Skinner |

**OFF-BROADWAY**

| | | |
|---|---|---|
| CHRISTINA ALBERTA'S FATHER | Fay and others | The Vineyard Theatre |
| ANGRY HOUSEWIVES | Various | Minetta Lane Theatre |
| PERSONALS | Various | Paul Lazarus |
| BLUE PLATE SPECIAL | Ramona | Manhattan Theatre Club |
| JUST SO | Elephant Child | Julie Ann Boyd |

**STOCK & REGIONAL THEATRE**

| | | |
|---|---|---|
| HAPPY END | Sister Mary | Baltimore Centre Stage |
| SWING | Female 2 | The Stevens Center, NC |
| PUMP BOYS & DINETTES | Prudie | Virginia Stage Company |
| STATE FAIR | Barker | Randy Skinner-LBCLO |
| PAL JOEY | Gladys Bumps | David Steinberg-LBCLO |
| A CHIRSTMAS CAROL | Mrs. Crachit | Long Beach CLO/Pitts. CLO |
| ME AND MY GIRL | Sally | La Mirada CLO |
| CHESS | Florence cover | Long Beach CLO/Pitts. CLO |
| GUYS AND DOLLS | Adelaide | Terrence V. Mann-NCT |
| ELMER GANTRY | Maude/Sharon | David Bell-Ford's Theatre |
| IS THERE LIFE AFTER HIGH SCHOOL? | Various | David Bell-Ford's Theatre |
| GREASE | Frenchy | Westbury Music Fair Tour |
| DOC AND LOLA | Marie | Lenox Arts Festival |

**TRAINING**

| | |
|---|---|
| **DRAMA:** | B. A. North Texas State University |
| **ACTING:** | Harry Mastrogeorge, Michael Howard |
| **VOICE:** | Joan Lader |
| **DANCE:** | Chuck Kelly, Randy Skinner |

Your tape shouldn't last longer than ten minutes, and unless you have a lot of experience, it will be difficult to bring it up to three to five minutes. Don't worry—most casting directors will know within the first couple of minutes whether they are interested in you. Chose only your best scenes, and start out with a punch. If you have plenty of clips, show as large a range of roles as possible.

Include your name and numbers, as well as a still image of yourself at the beginning and end of the tape. Your movie scenes should appear first, then television, industrials, and lastly commercials. Never include videotape of stage performances or home footage of you reading a monologue.

Editors can include a frame pause that states the name of the show (or commercial, or movie), the director, and your name and character name. It's almost always a good idea to acknowledge the director, both on your resumé and on video. Directors have lots more prestige and name-recognition than you do, so why not take advantage of it?

If you don't have much experience, you can include *professional-quality* footage from student movies. These jobs don't normally pay (except for transportation and meals) but you can ask for movie clips and assemble quite a nice group of diverse roles for your tape.

If you plan out the order of scenes beforehand and time them, it will make the editing process much quicker and cheaper. Almost all casting personnel and directors will take time to look at a tape, so you will have a powerful marketing tool for only about $300.

### Distribution

To distribute your tapes, print out labels with your name and contact numbers, and your agent's name and number. You can also affix a photo-postcard to the cassette box. It's best if you can let the casting director keep your tape. You never know when she might say, "There was that young man six months ago who would be perfect... I think I have a tape around here."

When you get new photographs, you can send out mass

mailings to casting directors who regularly cast productions you would be interested in. Put your P&Rs in a large envelope marked "Photographs—Do Not Bend." Include a typed cover letter with each that consists of a short introduction of yourself mentioning work you've done for them or names of people who are recommending you. Request an appointment to audition.

After a couple of weeks, send out your postcards as reminders that you are interested in an appointment to audition. It's not a good idea to phone casting directors; they'll call you if they're interested. It's your job to keep sending photos that will spark their interest.

Even better than a general mailing is when you send your P&R to a casting director along with a short note: "I hear you're casting for *Summertime*, and I think I would be right for the part of Hilary." This gives you an extra edge since casting directors are constantly involved in casting specific projects.

Every month, send out your photo-postcards to pertinent casting directors, particularly to television and commercial casting directors. Some will call in tenacious actors simply because the regular arrival of postcards indicates you are serious about your career. They'll inevitably audition you for parts if your face and name are fresh in their minds. It also helps if you update your photo once a year; if your photo shoot was successful, you should have half a dozen shots that can be reproduced.

And finally, whenever you land a job, immediately send out photo-postcards to let everyone know. People in this business love to work with professional actors.

## Answering Machine Etiquette

Once you've managed to get a casting director interested in you, don't blow it by delivering a monologue on your answering machine. You've already gotten the interview or audition when somebody is calling; being cutesy or long-winded will only aggravate the busy production personnel on the other end of the line. Leave a pleasant, professional message that will leave a pleasant, professional impression with callers.

Also, check your messages often—every two hours if you want to truly stay on top of your career. In television and commercial work casting directors often call at the last minute because they are being pushed to find someone at the last minute.

# 3 | *Unions*

First, the facts about working as an actor. Of the 150,000 members of the three main unions who live in New York and Los Angeles, nearly 80 percent make less than $5,000 a year. Approximately 10 percent make over $25,000 a year, with only about 2,000 of those professional actors making more than $100,000.

In addition, this income is sporadic. If you're a Broadway dancer, don't expect to be making $950 every week for fifty-two weeks out of the year. You may only get five weeks of pay one year, and twenty the next, then fall back down to ten weeks.

The union involvement in the acting industry varies from city to city depending on the type of work (specifics are covered in the chapter 7). By joining a union an actor gets the protection and benefits that the organization offers, but joining won't help you get work if you've merely bought your membership rather than earned it. In addition, it's much easier to get work as an inexperienced actor on non-union productions in some cities than it is in others. There is no "right" time to join; it depends on the work that is available to each actor in each location.

## Types of Unions

The *Associated Actors and Artists of America* is an umbrella organization that covers the three main unions for professional

24

actors: the *Actors Equity Association* (AEA or Equity), the *Screen Actors Guild* (SAG), and the *American Federation of Television and Radio Artists* (AFTRA).

Equity has jurisdiction over performers and stage managers in live theater. The Screen Actors' Guild covers performers in film and commercials. The American Federation of Television and Radio Artists works with live and taped television (soap operas, TV movies, commercials), and radio performers including actors, singers, dancers, disc jockeys, talk-show hosts, stunt people, sportscasters, and news broadcasters.

Additional unions include the *American Guild of Musical Artists* for musical and theatrical performers and the *American Guild of Variety Artists* for mimes, comedic performers, and magicians.

The unions are run by boards of directors whose elected members are volunteers and serve with no salary. Ronald Reagan was the president of SAG (1947–52 and 1959–60) and look what that led to! Under the board's direction, the policies of the union are then carried out by a paid staff of executives.

## Membership Benefits

The unions regulate the actor's business relations with the industry. They bargain with producers, networks, production houses, and ad agencies to establish minimum salaries for actors known as scale. For instance, current union scale dictates: $504 for a day's work in movie; $435 for a principal role on a half-hour soap; $415 for a TV commercial; and $950 for a weekly salary in a Broadway show. However, there are so many codes and types of agreements that the dollar amounts listed in this book are only estimates to help you compare the different types of employment.

Some union contracts are renewed each year, while others are on a three-year cycle. Since fees are negotiated, they can change dramatically within a few years, depending on demand.

The unions control the distribution of residual checks in payment for each appearance of an actor's work. Residuals are a result of union efforts to ensure that actors are financially rewarded when their work is shown in re-runs.

Unions also franchise the good agents, and only union members can only work through those that are affiliated. Unions also provide group health insurance plans for their members, pension plans, and cost-of-living adjustments. Union contracts dictate an actor's working conditions, such as date of payment, length of rehearsals, meal periods, place of rehearsal, time between calls, transportation, and performer safety.

If a union member has a complaint, the matter can be handled in secrecy by the union so it will not affect the actor's future employment. If a member violates a contract, they can be fined.

For actors looking for work, the unions provide national and local publications covering union activities, as well as workshops, talent showcases, lists of franchised talent agents, upcoming productions, and pending legislation. They also provide hotlines and bulletin boards, known as *callboards*, listing current casting notices.

## AFTRA

ADDRESS: 260 Madison Ave., New York, NY 10016

AFTRA and SAG have locals or branches throughout the country (see the chapter 7 section for these addresses and phone numbers.) In many cities these two unions are merged or housed in the same building.

AFTRA is an open union, which means that any actor can sign the membership application and pay the initiation fee to join. In New York and Los Angeles, the fee is about $800. Dues are paid semiannually on a sliding scale based upon the previous year's income. A new member pays the lowest amount (in New York, for example, it's $35).

Membership is mandatory if you work more than thirty days in television or radio on union jobs.

# SAG

ADDRESS: 5757 Wilshire Blvd., Los Angeles, CA 90036

If you have been a member of either AFTRA or Equity for a year, and have worked as a principal a least once in either union, you are eligible for membership in SAG. Your membership will also be accepted if you have a commitment for a role as a principal in a movie, commercial, or television.

The initiation fee is around $1,000, with semiannual dues of approximately $45.

## Working in Film

The Screen Actors' Guild covers motion picture work. Scale is the same whether the movie is a multimillion dollar movie or a local union production.

*Day players* are actors with bit roles that work for only part of the production period. The pay for one day is $500; for one week it is $1,750.

Extras earn $99 per eight-hour day. Stand-ins are used in place of the principal actors when the crew is lighting and marking the set. Both stand-ins and actors with special skills such as playing tennis in the background or Rollerblading past the restaurant are paid $110 a day.

Actors receive residuals each time their movie is televised. Videocassettes (rental or sale) also generate residuals, which is increasingly becoming a lucrative payoff for working actors. The residual percentage for the different types of acting work is negotiated by SAG. These residuals vary depending on the production and distribution contract.

## Television

Taped television shows are usually covered by AFTRA, though SAG has some jurisdiction over shows that are produced in their facilities.

Films made for television pay the same rate as motion

pictures—$500 per day for day players, and $99 for extras. For a television series, extras receive $99 for half-hour long shows and $125 for hour shows.

On daytime television soaps, the contract players portray regular characters in the series. These actors have work every day on new scripts in order to keep up with the production of a daily half-hour show. It's tough work, but the money is good. Contracts are negotiated for each actor depending on their popularity and the needs of the storyline.

Day players receive $435 for a half-hour show and $600 for an hour show. Bit roles or under-fives, (the actor has less than five lines) are paid $200 on half-hour shows and $250 for hour shows.

Any role on a prime-time series is considered a principal rather than an extra or bit part. Day players earn $500, three days are $1,250, and the weekly rate is $1,750. Actors who are hired for their special skills receive $200.

## Commercials

Television commercials are covered both by AFTRA and SAG. You don't have to join the union for your first commercial as long as you are hired for a principal part. If the casting directors have auditioned enough SAG people, they can file for a waiver for you.

However, you must join the union if you are booked for another commercial. And the union doesn't allow waivers on the first commercial for actors who are hired as extras. If you can get work as an extra, union membership may pay dividends in the long run. Extra work is an excellent way to get to know the directors, casting directors, and advertising executives which you need to impress in order to get cast as a principal on more commercials.

A principal—an actor who may or may not have lines to speak—earns $425 per day, per commercial. But the big money in commercials comes from residuals. Every time the commercial is shown, the actor receives payment. How much depends on the size of the market, the number of uses within a thirteen-week period, and where the commercial is placed in the programming.

Extras who are used in the background to flesh out the setting are paid $140 (which includes thirteen weeks of use). Unlimited use pays $240. If the director chooses to make you identifiable (either has you hold the product or use it), the residuals are the same as the principal actors.

Voice-over performers receive $300 per day. Hand models receive $375 per day for unlimited use, or $250 for thirteen weeks of use. For infommercials, scale is set at $900 for the first day, and $450 for each additional day.

## Industrials

Industrials are movies used in corporate training, motivational courses, and for sales and marketing purposes. Actors can find plenty of job opportunities in this part of the business, with roles as diverse as a mail carrier in a post office training video and performing a product demonstration for objects like a carpet cleaner or a water purifier to be shown on monitors at trade conventions.

If the movie is for corporate use, principals are paid $375 per day, $950 for three days, and $1,300 for a week. On-camera spokespeople earn $700 the first day, and $375 per day after that.

Industrials created to be shown to a general audience, such as the saftey videos shown on airplanes, pay actors slightly higher fees. Principals earn $475, three-day players $1,200, and a week's work pays $1,700. Spokespeople earn $800 for the first day, and $475 for each day after that.

In both forms of industrials, voice-over performers are paid approximately $300 for the first hour, and $90 for every hour after that. Extras earn $99.

For industrial shows, which often consist of work at conventions and trade fairs, scale for actors working two weeks or more is $875 per week, while those working one week receive

$1,100. The daily rate is $375 for the first day, and $180 each day thereafter. On occasion industrial shows travel for up to six weeks, and there is a per diem of $55 ot cover expenses in addition to the regular salary.

## Actors Equity Association

ADDRESS: 165 W. 46 St., New York, NY 10036

Equity is the union for stage actors. The four Equity office cities are in New York, Los Angeles, Chicago, and San Francisco. An Equity liaison city is an area with a minimum of 100 members and at least one Equity theater. Members of a liaison city elect a committee to act as a link between the local membership and the national and regional Equity officers.

If you have been a member of either AFTRA or SAG for a year or more and have performed work comparable to Equity principal work, you are eligible to become a member of Equity.

You can also earn your membership card by going through the Equity Membership Candidacy Program, earning work credit by performing in Equity theaters. These include Equity resident theaters, dinner theaters, and nonresident stock theaters, to name a few. By the time you accumulate fifty weeks worth of credit, you've earned your union card and built your resumé by working with professionals. You will also gain experience in the technical side of production.

Equity's initiation fee is about $800, and biannual dues are approximately $40. Members are also required to pay working dues of 2 percent of their gross earnings from Equity employment.

## Broadway Theater

The minimum scale for a Broadway show is $950 per week for actors, singers, and dancers. Rehearsal pay is the same as scale, unless the contract has been negotiated otherwise.

Chorus members who have lines or a specialty number (part of a song or a solo dance) receive $15 extra each week. Understudies who are cast members receive $33 additional pay per week for each role understudied. Understudies who are not cast members receive $950 per week, and may be assigned to understudy up to three roles.

Musicals tend to rehearse principals for nine weeks and the chorus for ten weeks. Dramatic plays may rehearse for up to eight weeks. Touring companies pay the same rate as Broadway, and there is also a per diem of approximately $80 a day.

*Special Production Contracts* are an agreement between the union and theaters with seven hundreds seats or less. Scale is $600 for a dramatic play. However this salary can be raised depending on the theater's weekly gross.

*The Theatrical Alliance* covers theaters and production companies that agree to lower ticket prices. It was started as a way to stimulate Broadway production by cutting union pay scales by 25 percent. Actors receive $713 a week and the top ticket price is $35.

*Letters of Agreement* establishing special provisions are sometimes created for individual theaters and productions in order to encourage the development of professional theater. The scale varies widely depending on the size of the theater, ticket price, potential gross, and number of performances.

*The Production Contract* is used by both not-for-profit and commercial producers—mainly Broadway shows, national and international tours, and bus and truck tours. It is also used for productions in performing arts centers as opposed to regional theaters.

The *Guest Artist Agreement* may be used by not-for-profit theaters or educational forums to hire a non-resident Equity actor.

## Off-Broadway

Off-Broadway contracts depend on the size of the theater and the level of its weekly gross. Minimum scale ranges from $600 to $625 per week. Rehearsal pay is the same as scale, and can last up to five weeks.

### Off-off-Broadway

Most off-off-Broadway plays are not union productions, with two exceptions.

Under *Equity's Showcase Code* for union sponsored showcases, tickets can be no more than $12 and actors are reimbursed for some expenses, though usually not more than car fare.

Under the *Funded Nonprofit Theater Code*, admission charge can be no more than $15 and performers are paid a stipend ranging from $140 to $750 per week based upon the size of the theater, potential gross, and number of performances. In theaters seating fewer than ninety-nine people, the salaries range from $200 to $300.

### Regional Theater

More than seventy-five theaters across the country are currently operating under the *League of Resident Theaters* (LORT) contract. Successful productions sometimes move to New York and Broadway fame (and Broadway scale). Many professional stage actors rely on regional theater to survive, both artistically and financially.

Sometimes LORT contracts are used for an entire company that is rehired seasonally. However, most actors are contracted on a show-by-show basis. There are five categories of contracts based on the weekly box office gross receipts averaged over a three-year period for each theater, that dictate salary and requirements. The LORT scale ranges from $425 to $550 a week, and the theaters often provide housing at no cost to the performers.

The *Small Professional Theater Contract* is used by both not-for-profit and commercial productions held in theaters with less than 350 seats (outside of New York, Los Angeles, and Chicago).

The *Letter of Agreement* (LOA) is an arrangement made

between Equity and a developing theater which hasn't yet grown into a standard Equity contract. Each LOA varies depending on the size, location, and gross receipts of the theater, and they often vary from year to year.

The *Members Project Code* is used in Equity Liaison areas, and is for member-produced projects. The actors involved are considered to be, as a group, the producer of the production.

### Summer Stock

Summer stock is one of the premier training grounds for actors. Participants usually have to learn eight plays in eight weeks, forcing actors to broaden their skills and learn how to work under pressure. Actors also get exposure to live audiences and professional production companies.

The *Council of Resident Stock Theaters* (CORST) code pays actors according to the capacity and potential gross of their theater. Scale ranges from $450 to $550 per week. There is no per diem pay.

The *Council of Stock Theaters* (COST) contract is used for non-resident stock actors, both musical and dramatic, participating in a production without a fixed troupe for the season. These commercial and/or not-for-profit theaters often star popular television and movie actors in established plays. Stars are paid by contract basis, and union scale for principles ranges from $450 to $550 per week. Actors are also given a daily per diem.

### Industrials

Also known as business theater, an industrial play is produced by a corporation and performed for an invited audience of employees, dealers, or buyers. Often a relatively well-known actor is used as the host and becomes associated with the company's product through advertising and infommercials.

Scale for actors working two weeks or more is $875 per week, while those working one week receive $1,100. The daily rate is $375 for the first day, and $180 thereafter. Sometimes industrial shows travel for up to six weeks, and there is a per diem of $55 to cover expenses.

# 4 | *Interviews*

A big part of being a working actor is getting to know the people who are hiring. Keep track of who you meet and audition for, whether they are casting directors, agents, personal managers, directors, producers, or writers. Talk to other actors and get their first-hand opinion on interviewing and auditioning for these industry professionals.

When you interview, don't try to impress people with who you are or make up false connections. Do make an effort to find out about the interview. If you engage him or her in a genuine dialogue, you should be able to discover things about his or her personal life that will create a bridge between the two of you (such as that you both have family from the same town in Pennsylvania or both went to college in New York).

Don't rely on tidbits of gossip you pick up in the trades to create rapport. Other people will use those things, too, and they are sometimes distorted or flat-out wrong. Instead, focus on anything that you draw forth from your conversation, creating a connection that will make you stand out from other actors.

Don't monopolize the interview. Some actors make the mistake of being so excited to finally be in the door that they talk non-stop, trying to convince the director or agent that they are the new rising star. The best way to impress people is to listen to what they want, then quietly re-sum up what they are

34

looking for in order to assure them you understand what they said. Then affirm that you can do the job. You don't have to convince him or her; you simply must be sure of yourself.

Basically that's what all agents and casting directors are looking for: actors who are poised, self-aware, intelligent, and able to take direction. They won't recommend an actor who makes his or her five-minute interview so strenuous that they let out a sigh of relief after you're gone.

It also doesn't do any good for you to try to catch the attention of agents and casting directors by sending kitschy gifts or singing telegrams. Usually such gestures impress people with your desperation rather than your talent. And if you do find the rare director who remembers you from your gimmicks, you still won't get a job unless you're perfect for the role. Everything else is simply a waste of your money and their valuable time.

If you do send something to a casting director if, for instance, you're being considered for a part and want to thank them for their recommendation, then make sure it's something tasteful, like a plant or potted flowers. Don't ever send balloons, gift baskets, food of any sort, liquor, mock-newsletters or magazines featuring you, or tacky souvenirs.

*A few other interview don'ts:*

Don't act rushed but don't overstay your welcome. A long interview is not necessarily a good one.

Don't fake admiration or assume friendship. Be yourself and enjoy the interview on its own merits.

Don't allow distractions to disturb you. Of course, the ideal interview would take place in a quiet inner sanctum where your light can shine with all its glory but it never happens that way. Work with whatever situation you are given, and always be gracious.

Don't give the interviewer your life story. Stick to concise answers to their questions, and let just enough of yourself leak through to tantalize them.

Don't give your age, but your age range. Keep it to within two to five years of your true age.

Don't preface everything with "I think" or "I guess." Be sure of yourself. If your opinion is asked, be truthful with a positive slant. For example, if the interviewer expresses admiration for a teacher you didn't get along with, don't launch into a tale of your personal woes, but agree with some insight that this teacher did give you.

Don't go into an interview when you're sick. Interviews can always be rescheduled, and if you miss the boat with this role, at least you haven't blown the chance of ever working with that casting director again by showing up with your eyes red and nose running, unable to speak because of your sore throat.

## Casting Directors

Casting directors hire actors, and as such, are contacts to be cultivated by you and your agent/manager. Many casting directors have a permanent position on the staff of a production company, packager, studio, network, or advertising agency. An independent casting director is employed on a per-project basis by the producer or packager.

Before you meet with any casting director, read the trades in order to find out what productions he or she has cast in the past, and which actors he or she has recommended. Casting directors are usually engaged in searches to find actors for particular roles, though they also make note of talent for future use.

Casting directors can have as little as two weeks to find actors to fill ten or twelve roles. Their choices are approved or vetoed by up to a dozen people, such as producers, directors, writers, and executives. This is where being listed in the industry guides is to your advantage. Many casting directors flip through the guides to get an idea of the type of actor they should audition for the job.

Often there are companies that perform the job of casting in the local area. Most casting companies that cast commercials or extras for regular TV series usually welcome new talent since their clients want to see fresh faces rather than the same pool of local actors over and over again.

Casting directors release breakdowns (usually through Breakdown Services) consisting of descriptions of the roles they need to cast for each script. For each role, anywhere from two to three hundred P&Rs are sent in by both agents and unagented actors.

To make general contact with casting directors, send in your P&R with a request for an interview appointment. Quite often independent casting directors will conduct a preliminary interview or prescreening, asking you to give a cold read of a part before bringing you in to audition. Auditions may take place in the presence of the director, producers, writer, or advertising executive. Often your audition is taped and edited before being presented to the executives.

With theater casting directors, you should send flyers of the productions you are currently in. Most of them like to see an actor on stage before they will recommend you to directors. Even if your production is at best lackluster, you can send a flyer with a note: "My big scene is during the second act. Thank you for dropping by."

Since casting directors are in hot demand by actors, don't let a slow or lackluster response stop you from pursuing them for work. They are usually under severe time pressure, so if someone wants to interview you for a part, then jump, even if it's at 9 A.M. on Sunday and you've been up all night bartending.

## Agents

Agents are in the business of selling talent to casting directors, producers, and directors. They encourage, nurture, and promote their actors. Yet the only one who can get you the job is you. The agent works for you, but you have to stay on the ball, generating leads and following up on maintaining relationships with people you've met.

Agents help you get auditions for jobs through their network of contacts within the industry, by consistently reading the trades, and by receiving Breakdown Services every day.

Agents submit P&Rs to appropriate roles being cast by casting directors. Then the agent does everything he or she can to get their actors an audition. If you are hired, the agent negotiates your contract and receives 10 percent of your earnings for that job. Legitimate agents are paid only by commission, never by fee.

Choose an agent who works with actors of your type (i.e. if you are a theatrical actor, then go with a theatrical agent). However it is possible to get an agent who is too overloaded with similar actors. If this is the case, you will rarely get called because the work is going to their other, established clients.

To find out about agents in your area, don't hesitate to ask other actors you meet. They can usually give you the low-down on at least a dozen of the local names. Avoid agents advertising in the want ads of the newspaper and don't aim for a William Morris agent right off the bat. Seek out the medium-to-large-sized agencies who are looking for new talent.

The question of whether to sign exclusively or freelance with an agent, or even whether to sign with a franchised agent or no agent at all depends on which city you work in. The options and then plusses and minuses are covered in chapter 7.

Agents must be truly enthusiastic about your talent and possibilities in order to sell your services. Good agents won't ask you to sign with them exclusively until they've seen you perform (on stage, in a private audition, or on videotape). Legitimate agents and managers will never ask you to read from a script, say that you have talent, then recommend that you take classes or attend a local school before they represent you. And you should never have to pay an agent an up-front fee to cover costs.

Legitimate agents will be licensed by the Department of Consumer Affairs, and the license should be displayed in the office. You can also check with the unions for lists of established agents.

### *Franchised Agents*

A franchised agent works with actors who belong to the local performers' unions. Actors may only receive work through an approved franchised agent if they belong to the union. It is the actor's responsibility to make sure the agent has been approved, though the union does provide a list of local agents.

Some agents specialize in a particular area, such as commercials or theater. The larger agencies usually have subagents specializing in film, television, commercials, and industrials. Franchised agents are an excellent source for actors breaking into film and television work.

Standard agency contracts approved by the unions last for one year. This gives you time to see if the agent is right for you, and gives the agent incentive to find work for you right away. After ninety-one days, if you haven't gotten fifteen days of work through an agent's submissions, either of you may terminate the agreement.

## Personal Managers

The personal manager, like an agent, markets talent to industry professionals. Personal managers aren't franchised by the unions or regulated by the state the way agents are, yet the Conference of Personal Managers serves as a board of ethics and standards, policing their own.

Managers work with agents, or directly with casting personnel, producers, and directors in order to get the actor work. However a manager can't sign a deal (only an agent can do that) and a manager takes up to 25 percent of your pay.

Managers often are involved along with studio executives and producers in packaging productions. Quite often they are influential people in the business who can turn their contacts and experience to good use for their clients. For an actor, a personal manager is most helpful when it comes to guiding a career further along its path, such as, if you reach a plateau and can't seem to move beyond certain types of work or roles.

Managers tend to have more time to devote to you than an

agent does and should be available for everything from intensive consultation on your image to career counseling. Since each manager has far fewer clients, he or she will be looking for scripts and roles that your agent simply won't consider you for because he or she has eight other actors who typically do that sort of role.

If you catch the eye of a personal manager, chances are you can be helped by the association. But don't just take his or her word for it; ask for a client list. No matter how impressive someone may sound, you are the one in charge of your career.

## Personal Publicist

Actors traditionally use publicity to draw attention to themselves, and once you have reached a certain level of success, a personal publicist can truly speed your career along. Publicists can help you develop media skills as well as trumpeting your accomplishments and activities to everyone in the business.

Publicists usually work on a monthly retainer ranging from $500 to $3,000. They do mailings and make phone calls to media people, obtaining interviews and arranging business meals. Do not get involved with publicists who rely on staged publicity stunts or flamboyant rumors—they will only undermine your credibility.

# 5 | *Auditions*

Learning how to audition successfully is essential to becoming a working actor. Your audition is your chance to show everyone what you can do. Yet you can't let yourself get intimidated by the opportunity and distract yourself from performing at your best.

The only way to give a good audition is by listening to your casting director. They know what the directors, producers, and writers want, and if you do what they say, you'll be hired. Many actors make the mistake of considering the casting director the enemy, as if they are someone to be fought or won over. Remember it only *feels* as if they have the power to crush every one of your hopes and dreams.

In reality, casting personnel are very, very busy people whose jobs depend on finding actors who can fill the roles. They want you to be good. In fact, they want you to be great, and they'll do everything they can to help you satisfy everyone.

## Be Prepared

No matter how right you are for the role or how good your acting technique is, you can't lose sight of the fact that acting is your profession. You must do your homework for each and every audition in order to be prepared.

First, determine if you are doing a reading or an audition. A reading is not a performance, and though you can familiarize yourself with the script, you shouldn't memorize it. It helps if you can invest in classes on cold reading. These classes will teach you how to give a read-through that casting directors want to hear while staying flexible enough to take direction.

Often the first reading is done cold at the interview in order to give the casting director an instant impression. Don't bend your head and bury it in the script. Look at the lines, then make eye-contact with your reading partner, or the casting director. It's considered good form to ask the casting director if you can look to them while you read your part. Some casting directors refuse while some will suggest you look to their assistant so they can better observe you.

When you're auditioning for any television or film role, you are entitled to have access to the script twenty-four hours in advance. It is extremely important that you go to the studio to get the script the day before your audition so you have time to get to know the part. Amazingly, many actors don't take advantage of this simple, sure-fire way to give an impressive audition.

Sometimes you might have to read the script in the casting director's office, or take it to photocopy it. Or you might have to go to the production office to get a copy. No matter what it takes, this will be time well spent. Your seriousness will do more. to endear you to casting directors than any talent you may possess, and even if you don't get the job, they will certainly call you back for more auditions.

When you get the script, don't just memorize the lines, become completely familiar with the character you are auditioning for. Think about the other scenes as well as the one you are scheduled to read. Consider the character's background—family, friends, work, and emotional and physical state—in relation to the other characters.

If you have questions before the audition, you can usually call your agent for clarification. If you are truly confused about the character or scene, then you can call the casting director. Either they or their assistant will be able to give you the information you need. They want you to be good, and they respect actors who are professional enough to prepare themselves before appearing for their audition.

Finally, when you audition, always hold the script in your hand even if you know it backwards; this will alert the casting director and everyone else in the room that you know you are not presenting a finished performance. It makes you look professional and open to directorial advice.

## Be Relaxed

Don't go into an audition thinking that this will be "the one"—the one audition that will make or break you, the one audition that will give you that necessary job. Do not audition as a means to an end. There will always be more auditions in your future, for roles bigger and better than this one.

The key is to give it everything you've got, and enjoy performing the scene for itself. You have to love auditioning or no casting director will believe you love performing and without that driving passion you won't ever be hired.

Think of each audition as a chance to get feedback to improve your next performance. That way, the experience will be satisfying on its own merits, not on the basis of whether or not you got the role.

Whether it's an interview, reading, or full audition, make plans for later—dinner, movies with friends, something where your performance isn't the center of your universe. That way there's something that you can mentally segue into rather than having everything begin and end with this one audition.

And keep your sense of humor. Most likely you won't be right for this role, but if you can impress the casting director with your self-possession, he or she will actively work to find a part that is suited to you. It may be next month or even next year, but you will eventually get called back for another audition.

## Rejections

If you hang your entire career on each audition, fairly soon the process will seem so weighty that you'll start to think you'd rather be a waitress for the rest of your life than enter another room where four bored people are more interested in thinking about getting home than listening to you.

That's enough to make anyone quit acting. Yet as long as you enjoy yourself and are content with your own performance, the reactions of your audience will only matter as much as they provide insight into what you could do better in your next performance.

Quite often casting directors report that the final choice for a role doesn't come down to who is the best actor; usually several of the final contenders could do the job well enough. The decision is based on terribly small things, such as the color of the leading actor's hair. If there are only three men in the show, all of them with black hair, then the blond man whom you auditioned against will probably get the part.

When the rejection does have something to do with the actor, it's often because they have played it safe and performed in a neutral (i.e. boring) way. Casting directors see so many actors every week, with dozens reading from the same script, that you must stand out in some way. Take a risk. Create something out of the lines you are given. If it doesn't work nine out of ten times, there's still that one time it inevitably will. Even if your interpretation is wrong, it will be memorable.

Another way to invite quick rejection is to be unprepared. Casting directors aren't impressed by lengthy preparations after the actor has entered the room. Or when the actor forgets his or her monologue or hasn't studied the script. No one succeeds at an audition by winging it.

Keep in mind the difference between a cold read and an audition. When you give a reading you aren't expected to memorize the lines until they're set in stone. Actors aren't hired because they are able to do a reading without the script but because they show an understanding of the character needed for the role. Perfecting the lines can come later.

## Don'ts

Don't be late. This is not only unprofessional, it is irritating to busy casting directors. They will remember and they will not forgive. If you are going to be late or will miss your slot entirely, call beforehand to let the casting director know.

Don't go to extremes when you dress the part. If you are being considered for a part in *The Grapes of Wrath*, that doesn't mean you should come in with straw in your hair. And don't use props to try to create the character. Wear simple, nice clothing unless you are up for a business-related job, in which case you should wear a suit.

If you are brought in for one part, don't insist that you're right for another one. That's the casting director's decision, and insisting that another role is better for you is a sure way to convince them that *this* role isn't right for you either.

If you think the lines for your role are terrible, very likely the casting director knows it better than you do. Don't criticize the material—it's up to you to make the best of what you have to work with.

When you are in the middle of a reading and you've gotten off to a bad start, don't keep muddling through the next two pages. If it isn't working for you, then you'll know it. Immediately stop and ask if you can start over again. Then get it right, or at least do the best you can on that run-through. You may get direction and have another chance.

When you are done, don't ever comment on yourself. This means you don't start analyzing your performance or even express by gesture—a grimace or hand motion—what you think of the audition. And don't maintain the character. Let yourself become neutral, then become yourself again when you thank the casting personnel for the opportunity to audition.

If you are told, "Thank you very much. Next..." don't ask "Did I do it wrong?" or "Was that all right?" These questions force the casting director onto the defensive, having to reassure you when you obviously aren't what they have in mind. You can ask, "Would you like to see it another way?" If they say no, thank them graciously for the chance to audition and leave.

If you are dismissed, don't insist, "Let me try again. I can do it better," unless you are convinced that you can make such a stellar change in your performance that it won't seem like the same reading. Otherwise you'll blow your chance to audition for this casting director again.

## Theater

When you audition for a theatrical role, listen to what the director says about the character and what he tells the other actors. Note the reactions of the auditioners. If you are unsure of how to interpret the character, then go with what you feel strongest. You can do the scene "wrong" as long as it's a clear performance. Then the director will know you can act, and it's only a matter of choosing whether to try to direct you.

As soon as you enter the stage for your audition, go forward and introduce yourself with a confident, assured manner. Make sure there is a distinct pause of transition before and after your scene. That doesn't mean you go through an entire warm-up on stage, or do a dramatic twenty second pause before you begin. Be neat and professional—a three- to five-second pause as you position yourself is more than enough. Then afterward, thank the audience, making deliberate eye-contact with the casting personnel, before exiting.

If anyone is interested in you, you'll probably be asked to adjust some aspect of your performance. This isn't a negative comment, but a technique that is used to determine if you are a skilled actor and can respond to input. The director wants to know if he or she will be able to work with you.

Many theatrical actors say that if you are called back, wear the same clothes you wore for the first audition. The theory is that since you've obviously hit the mark, why blow it now? Besides, the auditioners often make notes based on your clothing, for example "the girl in the black tights" or "the orange sweatshirt guy."

### The Script

For show-by-show auditions, you could be asked to read from sides of the script in production. The sides are a few pages pulled from the script, usually the major scene for the role you are auditioning for. You will receive the sides on the day of the audition. Arrive early so you have plenty of time to semi-memorize the lines and to develop your character. If the script is published (and most are), then you should study the role and the major scenes prior to the day of the audition.

When you receive the sides at the audition, think first about the broader points, such as movements—where does the scene start and where does it end? Who does the character interact with and why? What gestures can you make that will be few and succinct? Think about the scene with your entire body so you will be comfortable moving around on stage.

One of the quickest ways to grasp a character is to try to find the humor in the lines. Not that you should play the role slapstick, but a lightly humorous approach translates nicely into confidence, whereas you usually fall flat trying to be serious or tragic.

If the script of the play is in print, get it before the audition and study the role you want. You will probably be asked to read from the meatiest scenes, so work on your preparation. You ideally want to be able to read "off the page," which means you don't have to constantly refer to the script. And during your preparation, find at least two clear ways to bring motivational emphasis to the character. For instance, if you are auditioning for the role of Stella in *A Streetcar Named Desire*, you should consider that she threw off the facades of her Southern homeland, and sank to the baser level of Stanley, where sexuality reigns supreme. She would be uncomfortable with her sister Blanche and would try to be ultra-correct in order to appease her own sense of gentility. Feeling these emotions of guilt and shame will help you put fire into the role.

### Choosing Your Material

In open auditions, actors perform their own material, either in monologues or with a scene partner. This gives you a great deal of leeway as to what you can perform. But use common sense in making your choices. If your regional theater is doing six contemporary plays this year, don't memorize Shakespeare for your audition. Casting directors want to see actors in roles similar to what they're looking for. If you know which plays will be done, you can even chose a scene from one of them.

Also, if you're a late twentysomething, don't try to impress them with your versatility by performing the part of a grandmother. And don't perform in dialect—the producers need to hear your real speaking voice. You're up against enough obstacles, so cast yourself as ideally as possible.

Don't chose climactic scenes that need heavy emotion. Pick a quieter, transition scene when a revelation is made or an understanding is reached. Choose a piece that gives you some variety of expression, otherwise it's a one-note scene and the director will be bored after the first thirty seconds. And make sure enough information is imparted during the scene for it to be comprehensible. Does it create a sense of who, what, when, where, and why?

Stay away from overly familiar plays and monologues, especially those printed in books intended for actors. Casting directors have heard them all dozens of times before. Use obscure material such as early works from master playwrights, or plays that don't work as a whole but have magical scenes tucked into the acts.

During the scene, pare your gestures and movements down to the minimum. One of the biggest mistakes made by auditioning actors is to try to fill the stage with their energy. Quiet self-possession will focus attention on you much faster in exactly the same way people strain to hear a whisper and draw away from a shout.

### Monologues

If you consistently audition on the stage, you should always be looking for good monologue material. Always have two monologues thoroughly prepared. You may have as little as one day between casting notices and the audition, and a sure-fire way to kill an audition is to try to perform something you don't know.

The pressure of auditioning will be difficult enough without feeling as if you can't remember your lines. But it's more than just that—you should really know the part. Read the script and understand what the role is and where you are at in the character development during this monologue.

Prepare contrasting types of monologues. Actors sometimes choose a classic scene and a contemporary work (since 1960) or they pair a light piece with a serious one.

Short stories and novels are perfect for transforming into monologues but again, stay away from old favorites and monologue books. If a casting director has never heard your piece, that will give it twice as much impact. Otherwise you're competing with everyone else who has ever done the piece for that casting director.

You will be told how long you have to audition. If the time slot is three minutes, plan your monologue to last two and a half minutes. If you go over, you will irritate the auditioners, and will be cut off in mid-sentence. That's not the best impression you could make.

Some theater casting directors recommend that you keep monologues as short as a minute or minute and a half. It's difficult to convey much more than your quality with a monologue, and once the auditioners have that, they don't need to hear more.

As soon as you enter the stage, go forward and give your name. Then tell the audience the name of your piece, for example, "Act two, scene three from Mendal Williams's *Wait for the Last Time*." You don't have to build up the scene or describe the characters or the action. However you can give the date and location of the setting.

Some directors (like casting directors) don't like to be focused on by the actor. It makes it difficult to take notes, and they feel as if they must respond. If you do want to focus on a particular person, ask them, "Do you mind if I use you?" If they say no, then focus to one side of them so you are presenting a flattering, three-quarter view. Whatever you do, don't let your focus wander.

Your attitude before, during, and after the audition is as

important as your talent. Directors want to know they can work with you. The last thing they need to deal with is someone who's opinionated or difficult when they know they'll have fifteen other actors contending for their attention. Stick to the necessary information, don't ramble, and be prepared to start as soon as you enter the room.

## Film

Casting directors for theater and film are usually independent consultants. Read the trades and pay attention to the final credits of current movies to find out who's hot in the industry right now.

Before you go in for an audition, consult the Academy of Motion Picture Arts and Sciences to find out what movies the casting director, director, and producer have done before. Mentioning their past work (in only a positive way!) will help create a connection between you and them.

Also, ask around about both the casting director and the director (who often sits in on auditions) to find out what you can about their "auditioning philosophy." Some want actors to give an audition that pulls out all the stops, while others are looking for your ability to relate to the other actors or what you can draw out of the character.

Casting directors will want you to read from the script, though in Hollywood you often receive only a few pages of it to protect the secrecy of the project. If the part is small, it may only take one audition for you to get the job.

Actors who are being considered for principal roles will be called back for a screen test. You will get the sides a few days early so you can develop your character, but most importantly, listen to the direction you got during your first audition. What did they like about you? What sort of slant did they ask for in your first cold read? Expand on this direction.

The only time it's essential to memorize your part is when you're auditioning for a feature. It's the only way you'll be able to get away from focusing on the words and to give the director the nuances of your character in your movements and reacting off your partner.

## Screen Test

Don't expect the old studio production of a screen test, complete with cast and full wardrobe. Your hair and makeup will be done, you will be lit, and you will have plenty of chances to get it the way you want it, so relax.

There are classes you can take which will give you on-camera experience. These classes will allow you to assess your look on the screen objectively, and help you become more comfortable in front of the camera.

Find out which of the local classes are recommended by working actors and casting directors. As with anything else you're going to pay for, you have to be careful. The best classes are held at the most reputable schools, are given by experienced professionals, and at the highest levels of excellence only accept trained actors. Their focus is on enhancing your personal style and adjusting the techniques you've already learned for pre-senting yourself on film or videotape.

Since your appearance on the film clip is what will decide if you get the role, it's important to dress in a way that won't detract from your performance. Keep it simple: wear solid neutral colors. White glares, while black is too harsh against your face. Avoid bold colors, and if it's videotape, don't wear red because it tends to bleed around the shoulders.

Darker colors are slimming, while careful tailoring will minimize your flaws. Go for a smooth line and avoid tight clothing that will reveal every tiny bulge. The camera can add up to fifteen pounds, so women should wear skirts that come just above or below the knee, not miniskirts that will make you look hippy no matter how slim you are. Men should wear double breasted suits if a business look is sought.

The neckline of your shirt is the most important aspect of your clothing; it should frame and flatter your face. Jewelry should also be carefully considered. No earrings are better than tiny ones or styles that might clash with what the casting director has in mind. Avoid wearing multiple necklaces. The focus should be your expression, not your accessories.

## Television

Casting personnel in film and television are usually auditioning actors to fill specific roles and they need those roles filled *immediately*.

According to the requirements of SAG, the script should be available to you at least twenty-four hours before you are to read for a part. If it's an under-five you are often given the scene or even as little as three lines to read the day of the audition.

Make it your responsibility to pick up the script from the production desk and make use of your time to get to know the character. That doesn't mean, however, that you should overdo your method acting. Give a solid, bold performance and be ready to turn on a dime depending on the direction you get.

Again, dress plainly rather than rigging yourself out with props. That gives the casting personnel a chance to see what they want to see in you, rather closing all the doors. For example, you may think from the lines that they want a romantic, sweet young thing, when someone feisty and a little rough around the edges is what they have in mind. If you show up in ruffles with cute bows in your hair, you've blown it even before the words come out of your mouth.

### *Episodic Television*

When you talk to a network executive who supervises casting, make sure you know all of the shows that appear on that network. Prime time shows are broadcast one evening a week, while daytime dramas are shown five times a week during the day.

Find out which shows this casting director casts and become familiar with the name of the characters and actors, otherwise you won't be able to keep up a coherent conversation and the director will spot your ignorance a mile away.

Also, keep abreast of all the current shows enough to know

the basic plots, styles, and direction of the narratives. The only way to give casting personnel what they want is by seeing the type of actor they regularly hire.

If you can make an impression on a casting director who works in episodic TV, you are very likely to get a job. They need new actors for every show, and once you've been used on one series, it's quite likely you'll be hired to do something for another series on the same network.

Keep in mind that television auditions are difficult simply because of lack of time. It's exactly the same for the cast—they have less than a week to pull a performance together, whereas a film actor has three months.

### Under-fives

Even if it's only an audition for an under-five, take the time to investigate the show you're auditioning for. A small part can evolve into a principal character and generate a lot of work for you. (This consistently happens for bit players who make an impression on daytime soaps.)

During the audition play to the other actors, even if they aren't really actors. It's up to you to be the character, even if you only have one line. Fit your motivation into the rest of the storyline instead of making those few lines fit you.

Often you won't be right for the particular part, but if you can make an impression and take direction you will be called back to audition for other parts. When you audition for under-fives, don't expect to be called back for second auditions since one time is usually enough for them to know if they want you or not.

### Principal Parts

When you audition for day player or principal parts, you will receive the scene a day or two before the audition. If the director likes the first reading, you will be called back for another audition.

Callbacks are the second audition, when the lucky handful of actors who seem to be the best possibilities for the role are called back for a second look. Callbacks are when you can really put some work into your character, developing your own backstory to give it your personal spin. Also decide what your character was doing that morning, an hour before, a few moments before the scene. This will help you have an emotional understanding of the lines that will make your performance unique.

When you have a screen test, you will receive full makeup and will perform with the actors currently performing on the series. For soaps, screen tests are often done in between run-throughs and rehearsals for regular shows, which means there isn't a lot of time for the test. Yet these videotapes are vital to you as an actor because the executives will make their final decision based on your performance. You should also make sure to get a copy of the audition for other casting directors who ask to see you on videotape.

## Commercials

When you audition for commercials, you usually read from the script that is currently being produced. That means you have to be a fast study and be able to make sense of the character in a way that makes it you.

This is quite different from the small parts you audition for in a television series, where you must fit yourself to the tone of the series. Commercials are mini-plays with you as the star, and everyone from the creative director to the account executives want actors who can catch the attention of the audience.

Commercials are usually cast by advertising agencies. Your performance will be recorded on-camera, and callbacks are based on the results of the tape. At the beginning of the audition, you will be instructed to "slate" yourself, which is to say your name into the microphone.

Consider the slating process as part of the audition, the chance to make an impression of yourself without the burden of the copy on your shoulders. Don't go overboard—directors will fast-forward through your audition right from the slate if they don't like what they see. Key your exuberance only slightly higher than normal, giving them a chance to want more from you and then give it to them when you're performing the audition.

The best way to slate yourself is to simply say your name, "Tom Marcus." Don't giggle or show all of your teeth and say, "HI! I'm Tom Marcus." The director will be hearing the forced gaiety and a sing-song tone, and will know you're really feeling nervous as hell. Simply stating your name in a warm, affirmative way will attract the most attention. Also, give only your name, not your agent's name. Then wait a few seconds before beginning the audition.

The copy you read can range from brilliant to wretched, but it's up to you to bring a spark of genuine life to the words. Account executives look for actors who seem to *believe* what they are saying.

Read through the lines and come up with a few ways of saying them. This doesn't mean you overpower the script with the mood you've picked, but approach it from different ways. You may get a couple of tries while the casting director tosses directional adjectives at you.

### Cue Cards

Particularly in your first reading, it actually helps to *not* memorize the lines. You want to look as natural as possible, and there is an element to cold reading that brings a certain spontaneity to the words. Also, if you're nervously trying to remember the whole script, you'll look as if you're busy dredging up the next line while speaking the first words. You'll appear as distracted as you are.

Casting directors expect you to use the cue cards which are positioned next to the camera. When you read from a cue card, it appears that you are looking at the camera unless you shift your eyes to the lens. Even if it's only a few lines and you have memorized them, look at the cue card. Inevitably you'll forget the middle line if you don't.

Be comfortable and confident when you read the lines, and

don't worry about getting the exact wording correct. They are mainly looking for the gist of the script and the tone and feeling you eject into the words.

With the short amount of time allotted for the shooting of the commercial and with only a few seconds to make an impression, you have to be particularly flexible and fast on your feet. Listen to the writer, executives, and casting personnel for clues as to what they want, and don't argue motivation when you're given direction. With commercials more than in any other medium, time is of the essence.

# 6 | *Getting Noticed*

Casting directors and agents love to see actors in performances because it gives them the clearest picture of your capabilities.

Send out notices of your current work to relevant casting directors. If you are sending a flyer to a larger agency, then find out the name of an assistant casting director. They often have more time to see showcases and minor theater works.

## Talent Showcases

Talent showcases are an opportunity for you to perform and stretch as an actor and they are intended to lead to employment. However, most casting directors refuse to go to showcases that make actors pay to perform.

Before you decide to participate in a showcase, be sure the producer and director guarantee advance publicity. The program for the showcase should be ready two weeks prior to opening night so you can send them to all of your casting contacts.

The showcase program should also contain your bio and contact information. If contact numbers are not listed in the program, there should be an additional contact sheet that is distributed to audience members.

Some showcases prepare packages of each participant's P&R to be given to industry professionals who attend. Another important touch is a sign-in book, so that cast members can follow up by sending postcards to guests. That way everyone benefits when one actor manages to draw a casting director or agent to a performance.

### Finding a Showcase

The top-of-the-line showcases are mentioned in the Arts and Entertainment section of the Sunday issues of *New York* and *Los Angeles* magazines. You can attend local showcases to determine if you would like to be a part of a similar production and find out which casting directors regularly show up.

Usually you can get your foot in the door by volunteering to assist at a showcase first, either by ushering, doing stage work, or helping in the office. At the very least you'll be on the inside to hear about the next auditions.

Play readings can also be considered a type of talent showcase. There isn't as much production or rehearsal time involved as in a showcase, but it will give you a chance to be seen. Make sure you do your own publicity for play readings— usually they are presented by directors or playwrights who invite potential backers rather than casting personnel.

### Finding a Scene Partner

To find a scene partner, you should determine which of the people who want to participate are the best actors. Look at the experience and judge the chemistry between you and your potential partner. Then choose a scene based on these qualifications.

Teaming up with a poor actor won't make you look better, it will drag you down. Even excellent actors can't compensate when they're playing to a dead performance. Yet two pretty good actors can look brilliant if they work together and choose a scene that makes the most of what they've already got.

For example, say you're a rather "All-American football" type looking for a modern day Juliette, but the best actor in the bunch is a rather effete, middle-aged man. Go with the man, and find a scene that works with your types—it will be much more powerful that playing with a dead Juliette.

### When to Withdraw

Don't participate in a showcase that is filled with poor actors. Even if your scene is wonderful, the people you invite will be forced to suffer through an unpleasant experience and they won't remember you fondly for it.

If it looks as if a showcase will never shape up in time, then gracefully withdraw. You can always say you have other work or opportunities that you must pursue, and since participation is voluntary, there's no harm done. However, once the flyers are produced and distributed everywhere, then you must consider yourself committed. It's even worse if people show up to see you and you're not there.

## Amateur Plays

Many casting directors abhor to going to talent showcases, and much prefer to see a small cast performing a play for a few nights. Usually a group of actors serves as producers, paying to rent the theater for a short period and coordinating the stage management.

Casting directors will also go to see plays that are sponsored by colleges, universities, and accredited institutions. These have the benefit of giving you instruction while allowing you to be seen.

## Training

One sure way to catch the attention of casting directors and directors is through your training. Taking classes can be expensive, but training under a good coach will do more to impress a casting director than a long line of inconsequential credits will.

With many workshops and classes you can audit the class before making a commitment. For example, you want to be sure you're getting a good on-camera workshop that teaches more than giving a monologue on tape. You'll need to know how to hit your marks and stay on them during a complicated scene. In addition, small classes will allow you more time on tape and more intensive critiques that will allow you to work on any nervous gestures or mannerisms you've acquired and concentrate on moving within the role.

### Universities and Certificate Programs

Of all the universities and certificate programs that casting directors mention as impressive, there are some that are consistently mentioned.

In California: ACT in San Francisco, California State in Northridge, University of California, San Diego, and the University of Los Angeles. In New York: American Academy of Dramatic Arts, Juilliard, New York University, Herbert Berghof Studios, and the Lee Strasberg Theater Institute. A few in other areas are Carnegie-Mellon in Pittsburgh; Harvard; Yale; Northwestern; and LAMDA and RADA in England.

### Theater

For theater actors, a conservatory program is a wonderful place to learn your craft. A conservatory program is one where you're taught everything from dancing and speech to how to walk and research a character.

It may cost money, but if you can enter an intern program with a regional theater, you can get the experience you need and exposure to local casting directors. If you perform in regional tour, you'll meet every casting director at every regional theater, in-house. When these people like you, they will recommend you to casting directors in New York, Chicago, and Los Angeles.

## Networking

Networking is important for everyone in this business. Networking is not simply exchanging gossip, but keeping on top of current information and passing that information along. You can't network without giving because that's the only way you'll get others to give to you.

Part of networking is staying on top of what's new. Read the trade publications and know the names and productions as if they were being done by members of your own family. If you're a theater actor, attend and read plays—after all, your disinterest will show if you can't work at this job on the most basic level. The same applies to television and film actors—see the current work and keep up on which actors are being hired for what projects.

Networking will do more to create connections between yourself and professionals in the industry than anything else. As long as you are a member of the local acting community you have a much better chance of becoming a working actor.

# 7 | *Ten-City Acting Guide*

Where you live will help determine your success as a working actor. You don't necessarily have to live in Los Angeles or New York, but you do have to choose a city that has plenty of employment opportunities for your kind of acting. A serious stage actor may be happier in San Francisco or Washington, D.C. than in Miami or Philadelphia. And while LA is definitely the place to be for television work, Orlando has recently become a booming production site with its numerous sound stages at the MGM and Universal Studios theme parks.

Whether you prefer to work in theater, film, or television you can always find jobs in the three major show business cities: New York, Los Angeles, and Chicago. But if you want to lower your cost of living in order to focus on your career, there are seven other cities in the U.S. where a working actor can flourish: Boston, Washington, D.C., Philadelphia, San Francisco, Seattle, Miami, and Dallas.

In fact, it can sometimes be easier to get started outside of New York and Los Angeles, the two main hubs of the business. In the regional cities you'll find less competition, enabling you to launch your career or gain the experience you need to land better roles.

The ten-city survey in this chapter can help you decide which part of the country is right for you. The types of training and employment opportunities that are most readily available are listed, as well as valuable information on how actors can contact agents and casting directors. The local casting preferences and preferred experience are compared among the different types of work: theater, film and television, and industrials and commercials.

Also included are resource lists of everything you need to succeed in the business of acting: unions, professional associations, publications, training opportunities, networking sites, audition information, hotlines, talent books, and showcases.

Call to confirm the resource information such as phone numbers and addresses—like everything else in show business, they can change overnight. That's why you are referred to the trade publications in order to find more specific information on the hot talent agents, casting companies, and production houses. In addition, the number of union members in each area is rounded off, intending to provide an approximate comparison between the cities.

## New York

For many actors, the mystique and allure of New York makes it *the* place to be. There are more productions, more employment, and more diverse opportunities in this city than in any other. Of course, everyone who doesn't dream of moving to LA comes to New York, and that means the competition is particularly fierce.

In addition, the cost of living in the city is extraordinarily high. Yet for the price of sharing a tiny apartment with two roommates while working nights in restaurants and bars, actors in New York get more than the chance to make it big. They get to experience the culture of the performing and visual arts, music, drama, and experimental productions.

### *Training*

New York has the opportunities for you to study under some of the most respected teachers in the world. Classes are given on improvisation, voice, dance, movement, comedy, auditioning, on-camera auditioning, career management, and every acting technique ever invented. They also provide opportunities for actors to meet casting directors.

Some of the world's most renowned acting, dance, and music schools are in New York, including Juilliard, The Actors' Studio, The American Academy of Dramatic Arts, and The Neighborhood Playhouse.

Smaller private acting groups or not-for-profit schools regularly rise to notoriety for their innovative techniques, as with the Wooster Group in the '80s.

The trade publications run advertisements for smaller schools, workshops, and private coaches. It's best to check with other actors in order to assess reputations before handing over your hard-earned cash.

Another way of obtaining work is to take classes from theaters that have training institutes and internships. Again, check with locals to determine which theaters actually use their volunteer interns on the stage, and which use them as understudies, ushers, or production crew.

## Certificate and Degree Programs

The American Academy of Dramatic Arts
   ADDRESS: 120 Madison Ave, New York, NY 10016
   PHONE: (212) 686-9244

American Musical and Dramatic Academy
   ADDRESS: 2109 Broadway, New York, NY 10023
   PHONE: (212) 787-5300

Brooklyn College, Department of Theater
   ADDRESS: Bedford Ave. and Avenue H, Brooklyn, NY 10019
   PHONE: (718) 780-5666

Circle in the Square Theater School
   ADDRESS: 1633 Broadway, New York, NY 10019
   PHONE: (212) 307-2732

City College of New York, Department of Theater and Dance
   ADDRESS: Shepard Hall No. 229, 138 St. and Convent Ave.,

New York, NY 10031
PHONE: (212) 690-6666

*Fordham University,* Theater Arts Department
ADDRESS: 113 W. 60th St., New York, NY 10023
PHONE: (212) 841-5267

*The Juilliard School*
ADDRESS: 60 Lincoln Center Plaza, New York, NY 10023
PHONE: (212) 799-5000 ext. 251

*Marymount Manhattan College*
ADDRESS: 221 E. 71st St., New York, NY 10021
PHONE: (212) 517-0475 ext. 88

*National Shakespeare Conservatory*
ADDRESS: 591 Broadway, New York, NY 10012
PHONE: (212) 219-9874

*The New School,* Actors Studio
ADDRESS: 432 W. 44th St., New York, NY
PHONE: (212)757-0870

*New York University,* Tisch School of the Arts
ADDRESS: 721 Broadway, 13th Floor, New York, NY 10003
PHONE: (212) 998-1850

*Pace University,* Theater and Fine Arts Department
ADDRESS: 41 Park Row, 12th Floor, New York, NY 10038
PHONE: (212) 346-1352

### *Theater*

New York has such a huge number of theaters that they are separated into distinct categories. Broadway refers to the commercial theaters under Equity contract and/or theaters located in the Times Square area—from West 42nd Street up to West 59th Street, between 6th and 9th avenues.

Off-Broadway refers to not-for-profit theaters, or to smaller theaters under Equity contract (under 500 seats). Off-off-Broadway refers to not-for-profit productions held in theaters with less than ninety-nine seats.

Off-off-Broadway shows are often initiated by actors and directors as showcases, and are produced on strict budgets. Equity members may appear only in productions that operate under the union's NY Showcase Code.

### *Auditions*

Although Equity requires that its theaters hold open calls, actors are rarely cast in Equity theater productions in this manner, unless it is for a Broadway chorus. There is so much competition for Broadway theater that casting directors rely on agents to cull down the auditioners. If you have an agent, the best way to audition for specific theaters is by appointment for a particular show. That way you're reading from the actual script of the production rather than giving your own monologue.

Open calls are mainly used to cast touring companies, non-union theaters, dinner theaters, summer stock, cruise ships, and showcases. Unagented actors should still attend open calls at the Equity theaters because it is a good way to be seen. Hundreds of actors will arrive hours in advance for these auditions, so try to sign up for a slot where you can be seen early.

If the casting call takes appointments, by all means call to try to schedule yours as early in the day as possible. It's not true that the last people to audition remain uppermost in the minds of the casting personnel—by then they are dazed by a blur of faces and have been comparing the last nine-tenths of the actors to the first few that they liked. Even if you aren't right for the part and are auditioning just for the exposure, you have a better chance of being memorable if you are seen when the casting personnel are fresh.

When auditions are held by sign-up, an Equity monitor arrives an hour in advance to begin signing in actors for time slots. Actors frequently get on line hours early, then return later for their assigned time. Actors who show up after their names have been called can try to convince the monitor to work their name in.

For Equity chorus calls, the sign-up sheet is posted a week in advance. For non-Equity calls, often the first actor who arrives starts a sign-up sheet that the production staff may or may not honor. If you aren't sure, then remain until the monitor arrives.

### Film and Television

Most feature films and television shows are cast in New York or Los Angeles. The cities are seen as interchangeable, with LA based shows auditioning in New York and vice versa.

There is so much union extra work available in New York that some actors find they can support themselves just by doing that and the occasional commercial. Extra work is so good that there are casting companies that specialize in this area. These companies place notices for projects and general registration in the trades. You can send in your P&R at any time.

You almost always need an agent to audition for day player or principal roles for film and television. Only when a role is particularly difficult to cast will it appear in the trade publications. Independent nonunion projects do hold open casting calls, but without agent representation and union backing, you must be very careful about the terms of payment in your contract or agreement.

Publications such as *Performer Cues* list film and TV shows in pre-production, including the names and addresses of casting directors. You can always drop off your P&R, taking the chance you'll catch someone's eye at the right moment; however, most of the casting is done through agent submissions. Extra and under-five parts may come your way, which could lead to agent representation.

### Industrials and Commercials

New York is the business and advertising capital of the nation, so there's plenty of corporate work available. The Standard Directory of Advertising Agencies contains more than 900 listings in the city alone; and there are additional agencies in the tri-state area (New Jersey, Connecticut, and New York state).

Both commercials and industrials are usually cast through

agents, though casting notices for live industrials also appear in the trade publications. You'll find advertisements for dramatic actors, spokespeople, and even celebrity look-alikes.

On-camera work is rarely advertised, so it's necessary to work with an agent who specializes in this area. It often helps to get experience outside of New York so you have videotapes to show prospective agents.

Getting an agent who will represent you for commercials is easier than finding one for film and television. Most of the commercials are union, but you don't have to be a member to audition. Again, be cautious about nonunion projects—some pay slowly, if at all.

When it comes to commercial work, you will prosper if you can do a fair amount of self-representation. When you hear about a commercial being cast, drop your P&R off at the production house along with a note requesting an audition.

Once you've worked with casting directors, keep in touch by sending in updated photo-postcards. Once an actor is established in industrial work, the casting directors and even corporate production staff will often call actors directly to offer them work.

### Casting

New York is an ethnically diverse city, and every type of actor is sure to be in demand sooner or later. It's also the most color-blind city in which to work, since producers such as the legendary Joseph Papp, founder of the New York Shakespeare Festival, helped create the tradition of culturally diverse casting. In New York, you can also find constituent-specific organizations and support groups for almost every ethnic minority.

This is especially true of off- and off-off-Broadway productions. Theater on Broadway is much more conservative because of the exorbitant costs of producing a show and is therefore homogenized for the upper-middle class audiences, many of whom are tourists visiting New York. These more traditional stories tend to favor male characters, and middle-America facial types and physiques.

Industrials that are produced in New York require mostly white-collar corporate types and some blue-collar types. Live industrials are looking for a much wider range of characters, including actors with comedy, music, or dance skills.

### Networking

Since there is so much competition, networking is vital in New York. You have to get out there and meet people and actively pursue information that will get you auditions and job offers. You'll meet plenty of other actors standing in lines and waiting to see casting directors, so make the most of it. Be friendly and share what you know in order to get good tips in return.

You'll also get exposure by doing readings and other semi-professional projects. Actors are usually invited by the director or playwright to join in their productions, though occasionally auditions are held, particularly for showcases. Participation is a one of making new contacts and exchanging information about current work. For more information, you can contact playwrights' organizations and theater companies that special-ize in script development.

With the numerous universities and colleges in the New York metropolitan area, there are endless opportunities to be involved in student productions. Actors usually receive their meals and a videotape of the finished product in exchange for their participation. Members of SAG must be sure the pro-ducer/director has applied for a SAG waiver before committing themselves to a project in order to comply with union regula-tions. The waiver also ensures that you get paid in case the film gets picked up for distribution. Casting notices are run every week in Back Stage, and some are posted on the SAG bulletin board.

And of course, one of the best ways to network is to "hang out" in the restaurants that are frequented by other people in the industry. Even the poorest actor can afford a drink at the bar, and by talking to other aspiring actors you can find out the local diners and pubs where people gather. A few of the favorites are:

*Curtain Up*
   ADDRESS: 402 W. 43rd St., New York, NY 10036
   PHONE: (212) 564-7272

*Joe Allen*
   ADDRESS: 326 W. 46th St., New York, NY 10036
   PHONE: (212) 581-6464

*Orso Restaurant*
   ADDRESS: 322 W. 46th St., New York, NY 10036
   PHONE: (212) 489-7212

*Sam's Restaurant*
   ADDRESS: 263 W. 45th St., New York, NY 10036
   PHONE: (212) 719-5416

*Sardi's*
   ADDRESS: 234 W. 44th St, New York, NY 10036
   PHONE: (212) 221-8440

### *Talent Agents*

Agents in New York work on both freelance and exclusive levels. Freelance means that your P&R is in an agent's file and that you may or may not be called for auditions. If you're represented only on a freelance basis, it's best to keep pursuing leads until you're represented by several agents or until you find one who's interested in handling you exclusively.

The best way to contact agents is by asking for introductions from teachers and established actors. Then it takes work and perserverance on the actor's part to develop an exclusive representation with an agent. Consider the number of talent agents listed in the Yellow Pages to get an accurate idea of the amount of competition actors must work through.

Follow up every lead and referral you get for agents. This is one place where networking will come in handy. It helps to have some sort of recommendation because hundreds of people send in their P&Rs every week. Some agencies even post signs stating that they will not accept walk-ins.

Do your research in the trade publications to find an agent

appropriate for you. That way you won't waste time sending or walking in your P&R to agents who serve musical actors when you want to be in commercials. The larger agencies have agents handling each market—theater, film and television, industrials, commercials, and voice-overs—so address your P&R to the correct person.

If an agency expresses interest, it's usually up to you to pursue it. It's rare that an actor is ever courted. Don't let stiff telephone receptionists hold you off—it's their job to screen out all but the actors the agent wants to see. It's your job to make them know that the agent wants to speak to you.

### Casting Directors

Your agent will help set up meetings between you and casting directors. Many actors see casting directors repeatedly before they are used. It's important to maintain your relationships with casting directors; drop off new P&Rs and send flyers of your appearances.

Casting directors for networks, prime-time, soap operas, and advertising agencies are listed in the *Ross Reports* and other trade publications. You can send them your P&R or call for an appointment for an interview, but keep in mind that it takes work to land roles without an agent. However, should you get cast, you'll have no problem getting agent representation.

Some casting directors teach workshops and seminars about auditioning and in acting technique. Some are considered simply a way for actors to meet casting directors and are of dubious value. Sometimes acting showcases are announced, but require that you to pay to be included in a several person production geared toward performing for agents and casting directors.

### Unions

The best way to be seen in New York is to participate in the union showcases, auditions and open calls. Members are notified of job opportunities through newsletters and hotlines. Contact the local union that represents your type of acting (see chapter 3 for more details).

*The Associated Actors and Artistes of America*
  ADDRESS: 165 W. 46th St., New York, NY 10036
  PHONE: (212) 869-0358

*Actors' Equity Association* ("Equity")
  MEMBERS: 15,000
  ADDRESS: 1650 Broadway, New York, NY 10036
  PHONE: (212) 869-8530

*American Federation of Television and Radio Artists*
*(AFTRA)*
  MEMBERS: 21,500
  ADDRESS: 260 Madison Ave., 7th Floor, New York, NY 10036
  PHONE: (212) 532-0800

*Screen Actors Guild (SAG)*
  MEMBERS: 23,000
  ADDRESS: 1515 Broadway, 44th Floor, New York, NY 10036
  PHONE: (212) 265-3687

*American Guild of Musical Artists (AGMA)*
  ADDRESS: 1727 Broadway, New York, NY 10019
  PHONE: (212) 265-3687

## *Professional Associations For Performers*

  ADDRESS: 484 W. 43 St, #42A, New York, NY 10036
  PHONE: (212) 564-2485
    This organization provides support groups at no charge
for performers who are in vocational crisis. There is also a
"hospitality program" for former group members.

*Hispanic Organization of Latin Actors (HOLA)*
  ADDRESS: 250 West 65th St., New York, NY 10023
  PHONE: (212) 595-8286
    This organization serves as a support and information
center for Hispanic artists and works to increase an
awareness of their culture in the mainstream media.
Services include a newsletter, workshops, a talent directory, and a theater festival.

*Pentacle*
ADDRESS: 104 Franklin St, New York, NY 10013
PHONE: (212) 226-2000
    This organization provides support services in the form of publicity, accounting, and booking for dance and performance artists.

## Publications

*Back Stage*
ADDRESS: 330 W. 42nd St., 16th Floor, New York, NY 10036
PHONE: (212) 947-0020
    This weekly trade publication comes out every Thursday, and is available by subscription or at the numerous newsstands around the city. It is the primary source of audition information on the east coast, with a good number of the advertised auditions taking place the next day on Friday.

*New York Casting*
ADDRESS: 135 E. 65th St., 4th Floor, New York, NY 10021
PHONE: (212) 472-6585
    This biweekly publication is available by subscription or at newsstands and is distributed free at performers' organizations, schools, and unions. It provides casting notices and lists of agents, casting directors, production houses, and theater companies.

*New York Casting and Survival Guide*
PHONE: (212) 869-2020
(New York: Peter Glenn Publications)
    This guide is updated annually and lists all the services necessary to the acting community, including bookstores, talent agencies, vocal coaches, and wardrobe outlets, as well as a daily planner. You can find it in any of the industry bookstores listed below.

*New York City Geographical Casting and Agency Guide*
(New York: Pro-Labels)

.This guide is updated quarterly and provides lists of casting directors, talent agencies, and advertising agencies according to their location in the city. It also includes useful maps.

*Performer Cues*
ADDRESS: 1501 Broadway, New York, NY 10036
PHONE: (212) 997-1701

This weekly publication comes out on Tuesdays and is available by subscription or at newsstands. It provides casting notices and lists of agents and casting directors.

*Ross Reports Television*
ADDRESS: 40–29 27th St., Long Island City, NY 11101
PHONE: (718) 937-3990

This monthly booklet is available by subscription. It provides casting information for NY and LA television shows as well as information about NY commercial producers, talent agents, and casting directors.

*The Theatrical Calendar*
ADDRESS: 1780 Broadway, #300, New York, NY 10019
PHONE: (212) 245-1460

This biweekly publication lists shows under production on Broadway and off-Broadway. It also includes information for some regional theaters. It is available by subscription or in industry.

## Hotlines

*Equity Chorus:* (212) 869-8530

This hotline gives information on Equity chorus calls only.

## Bookstores

*The Actor's Heritage*
ADDRESS: 262 W. 44th St., New York, NY 10036
PHONE: (212) 944-7490

*Applause Theater/Cinema Books*
    ADDRESS: 211 W. 71st St., New York, NY 10023
    PHONE: (212) 496-7511

*The Drama Book Shop*
    ADDRESS: 723 7th Ave, 2nd Floor, New York, NY 10036
    PHONE: (212) 944-0595

*Theaterbooks*
    ADDRESS: 1600 Broadway, 10th Floor, New York, NY 10019
    PHONE: (212) 757-2834
    There are numerous talent directories advertised in New York, but you must make sure you aren't spending your money for nothing. It's best to have an agent advise you as to which books are reputable and regularly used by casting directors.

*Players' Guide*
    ADDRESS: 165 W. 46th St., New York, NY 10036
    PHONE: (212) 869-3570
    This talent directory has been around for years, and it only lists members of SAG, Equity, or AFTRA. If you are a member of the union, no matter which city you decide to live in, you should get yourself listed in the Player's Guide. When casting directors are need to cast a part, they often flip through the guide to find talent.

### *Talent Showcases*

*StrawHat Auditions*
    ADDRESS: P.O. Box 1226, Port Chester, NY 10573
    This general audition for non-Equity summer stock is held annually in March in New York City. Casting directors from Eastern and Midwestern theaters attend.

## Los Angeles

Los Angeles undeniably has the lead when it comes to moviemaking and television production. In fact, the city seems so full of opportunities that almost everyone, from kindergarten teachers to car mechanics, is writing a screenplay.

The city is also full of freeways—you have to do a lot of driving to get anywhere in Los Angeles. In New York, you could actually walk around the tiny world of acting contained within the 3 x 9 mile island of Manhattan. But in Los Angeles, the business is spread out in a network of production pockets— Hollywood, Beverly Hills, the San Fernando Valley, Malibu, and Orange County—separated by many miles and a lot of traffic.

Though the West Coast lacks the intensity of eastern culture—Manhattan is the focal point of both business and the arts—it does have long, white-sand beaches and plenty of sunny days. The dream of fast success and the warm weather draws thousands upon thousands of wannabes in every conceivable trade to LA, including thousands of actors who want to become stars. The cost of living in LA is slightly lower than in New York, especially south of the city in the sprawling suburbs of Orange county, but the amount of competition means that actors tend to have more time between jobs.

One of the biggest differences between the coasts is that in LA your appearance is more important than your training. Auditioning is more a skill of convincing producers that you are what they want than of impressing them with your acting technique. You have to be malleable and have endless optimism to survive the inevitable rejections for superficial reasons—too fat, too thin, too tall, too young, etc.

### *Training*

There are many schools, workshops, and private coaches in LA that cover every kind of specialty or discipline in the performance arts, from method acting to stunt work, from monologues to stand-up improvisation. Since actors are stringently categorized in LA, training mainly involves developing skills that will enable you to make a quick impression of your character.

You can find a list of private coaches in the *Acting Coaches* and *Teachers Directory*. In order to gain audition experience, you can also take on-camera classes given by casting directors. But don't be misled into thinking you'll make many legitimate work contacts that way. These classes are mainly for getting tips on your movements and appearance, including what makeup and hairstyle work best for you, as well as what types of clothing you should choose.

Actors who do take time to get certified training or a degree in some type of performance art from local programs are respected by the West Coast casting directors because of the high quality of the teachers. Daytime soaps in particular tend to hire theatrically trained actors because they have been taught stamina: how to give life to a character day after day.

## Certificate and Degree Programs

*American Academy of Dramatic Arts*
ADDRESS: 2550 Paloma St., Pasadena, CA 91107
PHONE: (818) 798-0777

*California State University,* Department of Theater Arts
ADDRESS: 1250 Bellflower Blvd., Long Beach, CA 90840
PHONE: (213) 985-5357

*Loyola Marymount University,* Theater and Dance Program
ADDRESS: 7101 W. 80th St., Los Angeles, CA 90045
PHONE: (213) 338-2837

*University of California,* Theater Department
ADDRESS: 405 Hilgard Ave., Los Angeles, CA 90024
PHONE: (213) 206-0426

*University of Southern California,* Division of Drama
ADDRESS: Drama Center, Los Angeles, CA 90089-0791
PHONE: (213) 740-1285

## Theater

Though LA isn't known as a theater town, there is plenty of stage work available. Since the 1988 Equity agreement went into effect with smaller theaters the Los Angeles ninety-nine-

Seat Theater Plan, Equity members can appear at non-union theaters with seating under ninety-nine people in exchange for expense reimbursement. This allows actors to showcase themselves and get experience outside of television and film jobs without losing their union membership.

Equity also has LORT contracts with about a dozen theaters, production houses, and special production houses in the southern California area. The Mark Taper Forum and the Ahmanson Theater hold a general audition every year, yet these theaters tend to use casting directors and agents to find most of their talent.

There are also a few theaters under the HAT (Hollywood Area Theater) contract for houses with no more than 399 seats. These theaters are more open to new talent than the LORT or production houses.

Check the publications for open calls—almost all theaters have them occasionally. The auditions are crowded, so show up early to sign up. The audition notice will specify if you will be asked to perform a monologue or read from the script. If the script will be used, then take the time to purchase it and get to know your character's most important scenes.

### Film and Television

You won't be able to audition for film and television roles without an agent. Even if you do have representation, you must do a lot of your own networking to make sure you're seen by casting directors, either on the stage, in showcases, or through agent submissions.

The pilot season, when new television series are traditionally being packaged and pitched to the networks, lasts from January to May. But pilots are being packaged year-round with increasing frequency. It's best to establish your contacts and make an impression in fall or early winter, *before* casting directors hit their crunch time and have no time to see you.

Once a series is established, it needs bit players all the time except for during the traditional hiatus during late spring and summer. To maximize your time, watch the shows and pick the ones that have bit players that fit your "type." Shows like *Melrose Place* and *Baywatch* want actors with young, striking physiques, while a sitcom like *Seinfield* features a new actress as Jerry's girlfriend virtually every week, and each one has her own unique twist. Then you can target the shows that suit you, contacting the casting directors and familiarizing yourself with the series in case you are called in for an audition.

You have to be aware of what character types casting directors want. If you're auditioning for a soap opera, they'll want a different sort of unwed mother than you would create for a thriller movie. Don't try to give them what you think they should have, but what the casting director has already shown a preference for. They know what's right for them.

Your ability to quickly read and grasp a character is essential for television work. Casting directors don't have time to coach you into the role. You have to give it everything you've got in order to *be* the character in the audition.

You will usually read sides at an audition. Either your agent will provide the script for you, or you can arrive the day before to get the script.

First and second readings often aren't videotaped, but find out for sure in advance so you can prepare your look for the camera if this happens to be the exception. If you're told it's "no makeup" you're being asked to present a natural image. Naturally, you must wear some makeup for camera work. Women in particular are expected to present a stylish, neat appearance, while male actors have been known to audition in jeans and a t-shirt.

### Industrials and Commercials

Though there is a thriving corporate market in LA—some say the best in the country—you don't hear many actors talking about their industrial work. Industrials just aren't glamorous enough to be taken seriously in this image-conscious city. However, this kind of work can pay the bills if you are represented by a good industrial agent.

In LA, commercials are considered to be several notches

higher than industrials status-wise. Many commercials hire "characters"—moms, kids, people with unusual and/or striking features—for memorability. Yet more than enough "beautiful people" and even stars are regularly hired to give the products in commercials a good name. The LA setting—the palm trees, beaches, and Rollerblading Americans—draws commercials from all over the world.

There are only a handful of top commercial agencies. Talk to other actors and casting directors to find out which ones have the best reputation. Once you've met a casting director for commercials, it's essential to stay in contact. Casting directors often contact actors directly for spot auditions.

The voice-over market is also good, particularly in the growing animation business. Cartoon work can be quite lucrative.

### Casting

In LA, you must discover what types you fit in order to successfully pursue employment. As always, appearance is nearly everything in this city. If you are the perfect cowboy, then you'll find cowboy roles. If you look like Elvira, however, you better reconcile yourself to not finding many soap opera parts.

Minority actors finally are getting plenty of access to work in television series. There is also a higher percentage of women's roles in LA than in New York, but most of these are under-thirty roles. The disparities between male and female salaries among star players (according to SAG statistics) are shocking.

### Networking

With such fierce competition, it's important to generate connections and personal recommendations for agents, producers, and casting directors. There are lots of beautiful people here, so you need something extra to catch people's attention. A warm and outgoing personality can make a world of difference for your career.

You can make an impression simply by being seen at parties,

openings, and local hot spots. Remember that old story about the movie star being discovered at the lunch counter in Schwab's Drugstore? The same principle still applies.

The hot places to see and be seen include health clubs, sport clubs and bars, parties, and restaurants. Some restaurants are quite expensive, such as the City Restaurant, Morton's, and Spago. Others that are more readily accessible are

*The Moustache Cafe*
 ADDRESS: 8155 Melrose, Hollywood, CA 90046
 PHONE: (213) 651-2111

*Residuals*
 ADDRESS: 11042 Ventura Blvd., Studio City, CA
 PHONE: (818) 761-8301

*Village Coffee Shop*
 ADDRESS: 2695 N. Beachwood, Los Angeles, CA
 PHONE: (213) 467-5397

## *Talent Agents*

Agents in LA are not known for their kind reception of newcomers. This is where your networking skill will be useful. As long as you have a contact name or recommendation, you will at least get in the door. If you've been working in another city under an agent, find out if the agent has ties to LA and can pass along your name.

Representation is usually on an exclusive basis. Many agents specialize in one particular area, however, so you may have one agent for commercials, and another for film work.

Agents are unofficially yet handily rated (A, B, C, D) in a local monthly publication, *The Agencies*. A and B agents have the best reputations in the city, but these ratings shift depending on who they are representing and what productions they are involved in. Other actors and publications will freely toss around these unofficial ratings, giving you an idea of the accessibility of the local agents. If you can't find representation with an A or B agent, a lower ranked agent, who may also be more open to new talent, can still help you build a resumé and get experience in the city.

Los Angeles is very camera-oriented, so it's best if you have a videotape of your work. Even a clip from a student film, so long as it has a professional look, will do fine. Don't offer a videotape of a stage production, home video, or anything amateurish. If an agent interested in your P&R, calls back, have a scene rather than a monologue prepared. For some reason, monologues aren't as popular in LA as they are in New York.

### Casting Directors

Casting directors invariably go through agents to find talent. The exception are the multitude of showcases that are given every month in LA. Be prepared to cultivate any casting director you meet, and send them your P&R and photo-postcards.

Casting directors change jobs a lot in LA, so you must work hard to maintain contact with those you have met. Television casting directors are the most accessible because they have dozens of bit parts to fill every week. Unfortunately, once you've appeared on a particular episode, you can't be seen in another part in the same series. That's why staying in touch as a casting director moves around is one of the best ways to get more than one role.

### Talent Unions

*Actors' Equity Association* (Equity)
  MEMBERS: 8,000
  ADDRESS: 6430 Sunset Blvd., Los Angeles, CA 90028
  PHONE: (213) 462-2334

*American Federation of Television and Radio Arts* (AFTRA)
  MEMBERS: 25,000
  ADDRESS: 6922 Hollywood Blvd., 8th Floor, Hollywood, CA 90028
  PHONE: (213) 461-8111

*American Guild of Musical Artists* (AGMA)
ADDRESS: 12650 Riverside Dr., Suite 205, North Hollywood, CA 91607
PHONE: (213) 877-0683

*Screen Actors' Guild* (SAG)
MEMBERS: 31,000
ADDRESS: 7065 Hollywood Blvd., 8th Floor, Hollywood, CA 90028
PHONE: (213) 465-4600

## Professional Associations

*The Actors Jam,* The Highland Grounds Coffee House
ADDRESS: 742 N. Highland Ave., Hollywood, CA 90028
PHONE: (213) 466-1507
This weekly, informal event takes place on Tuesdays at 8:00 P.M. It allows actors to present scenes and monologues, mostly from classical works, in front of the coffeehouse patrons.

*Nosotros*
ADDRESS: 1314 N. Wilton Place, Hollywood, CA 90028
PHONE: (213) 465-4167
This not-for-profit organization works to enhance the image of Hispanic actors. Services include the Nosotros Theater, talent showcases, workshops, and a talent book.

*Theater League Alliance* (Theater LA)
ADDRESS: 644 S. Figueroa St., Los Angeles, CA 90017
PHONE: (213) 614-0556
This organization is an association of independent producers and theaters in the Los Angeles area dedicated to development and growth of local performing arts. Services include a theater management library, a JobBank for the administrative and design aspects of theater management, and cooperative advertising. Interns are accepted.

*Women in Theater*
   ADDRESS: P.O. Box 3718, Hollywood, CA 90078
   PHONE: (213) 465-5567

   This organization is for both male and female actors who wish to "enhance our art form through education, interaction, and experience with one another." It offers an annual magazine, workshops, networking opportunities, and readings. Members' P&Rs are on file for the use of member directors and playwrights.

## Publications

   There are several trade publications in southern California that you should read in order to be aware of current and planned productions. These include *Daily Variety, The Hollywood Reporter,* and *American Film.* You can buy them at almost any newsstand in the local area.

*The Agencies*
   ADDRESS: P.O. Box 44, Hollywood, CA 90078

   This monthly publication is available by subscription or at the Samuel French and Larry Edmunds bookshops. It provides information about every agency, including the names of agents, union franchise status, types represented, along with useful commentary.

*DramaLogue*
   ADDRESS: P.O. Box 38771, Los Angeles, CA 90038
   PHONE: (213) 464-5079

   This weekly publication is available by subscription or at newsstands. It provides reviews, articles, advertising, and casting notices, particularly for non-Equity theaters, theaters under ninety-nine seats, student films, and auditions for nonunion TV, video, and film.

## Hotlines

*Actors' Equity Association:* (213) 462-2334
   Audition notices for members only.

Screen Actors' Guild: (213) 465-4600
    Audition notices for members only.

## Talent Books

Academy Players Directory
    ADDRESS: 8949 Wilshire Blvd., 6th Floor, Beverly Hills, CA 90211
    PHONE: (213) 247-3058
    The Academy of Motion Picture Arts and Sciences publishes this Directory, which is a must for anyone working in film and TV anywhere in the US. To be listed you must be a member of a union or signed with a franchised agent.

Women in Theater
    ADDRESS: P.O. Box 3718, Hollywood, CA 90078
    PHONE: (213) 465-5567
    Women in Theater maintains a P&R file of actors interested in participating in readings or for use by member directors and playwrights.

## Talent Showcases

AFTRA Showcase
    ADDRESS: 6922 Hollywood Blvd., 8th Floor, Hollywood, CA 90028
    PHONE: (213) 467-8702
    This showcase is held the first Tuesday of every month for actors to perform scenes for agents and casting personnel. Registration is on a first-come, first-serve basis.

National Alliance of Musical Theater Producers
    ADDRESS: 330 W. 45th St., Lobby B, New York, NY 10036
    PHONE: (212) 265-5376
    This New York organization also sponsors combined auditions in LA. You can call or consult DramaLogue for dates.

*SAG Seminars and Scene Showcases*
ADDRESS: 7065 Hollywood Blvd., Hollywood, CA 90028
PHONE: (213) 461-1023

The Casting Committee of SAG sponsors seminars including question-and-answer sessions with casting directors. Scene showcases are presented twice each month, and are jointly sponsored by SAG and the Casting Society of America.

## Chicago

Chicago offers a style of its own—a unique blend of East Coast sophistication with a dash of the down-home flavor of what was once a Midwestern cattle town.

Chicago is an easier town to survive in than New York or Los Angeles because the cost of living is much lower. The union states that per-capita earnings are higher in Chicago than in any other city, which means that there's more work for every actor. It's one of the only places in the US where actors can actually earn a living in the theater and is considered to be the nation's "second city" after New York. It is also one of the busiest markets in the country for industrials, commercials, and voice-overs.

The emphasis in Chicago is on acting, directing, and writing rather than on flashy production or lavish entertainment. Though actors are well respected in Chicago, it's still difficult to gain national fame or make large sums of money in this town. Many actors move on to New York or Los Angeles once they've acquired experience in Chicago.

### Training

Though the emphasis in Chicago is on the craft of acting, there aren't many additional training opportunities outside of the local universities and colleges (which are well-known for their drama departments). Perhaps this is simply because Chicago theater actors train as they work on the stage.

For independent study, there are directors and casting directors who offer workshops in a range of techniques, from voice-overs to formal training. The *Actors Center* provides courses in technique while *Act One Studio* offers workshops and private career consultations, particularly for actors who are new to the area.

### *Certificate and Degree Programs*

*DePaul University,* The Theater School
ADDRESS: 2135 N. Kenmore Ave., Chicago, IL 60614
PHONE: (800) 433-7285

*Northwestern University*
ADDRESS: 1979 Sheridan Rd., Evanston, IL 60208
PHONE: (708) 491-3210

*Roosevelt University*
ADDRESS: 430 S. Michigan Ave., Chicago, IL 60605
PHONE: (312) 341-3719

*University of Illinois at Chicago*
ADDRESS: P.O. Box 4348, Chicago, IL 60680
PHONE: (312) 996-3187

### *Theater*

Both *Steppenwolf* and the *Remains Theater* have been credited with creating the "Chicago style" during the late '70s. These acting companies supported non-traditional directors and actors who were experimenting with theater production (Steppenwolf took its name from the 1927 Herman Hesse novel about the social prejudices that an outsider must overcome in order to succeed).

This theatrical revival was admired by the entire nation and gave birth to well over one hundred Chicago-area theaters. Yet many actors complain that the city that once used to be the place for exciting, independent production has recently become relatively staid and complacent.

Currently the non-Equity theaters are considered to be the torch-bearers of innovative productions. Since non-Equity pay consists of stipends (usually too small to allow actors to be self-supporting without extra income) these theaters are able to operate on much smaller budgets and produce works that major companies couldn't afford to try.

Whether a company is Equity or non-Equity, the productions are covered and reviewed in the same way. What an actor loses in pay can often be made up for in prestige if he or she is noticed in a unique show.

There's also a great respect for actors who work their way up locally. So if you're a newcomer, it's best to begin in non-Equity productions before trying to get cast in Equity plays.

There are only two LORT theaters in Chicago, the Goodman and the Northlight. Most of the small commercial producers and not-for-profit Equity theaters use the tiered Chicago Area Theater (CAT) contract, which is similar to New York's Off-Broadway contract.

Sometimes the large New York musicals come to Chicago, and a few of the national tours originate in Chicago as well, but the casts aren't made up entirely of locals. The Goodman produces a musical every year, and there are a handful of dinner theaters which provide multistage productions with large casts.

A recent trend is to reproduce New York's hit plays in Chicago using a local cast. Some off-Broadway producers like to present their shows in Chicago in order to get a longer run before bringing their play New York.

### Auditions

Most of the theaters hold annual general auditions, usually between May and July. You can check the *Chicago Reader* for announcements, which includes the date and time you can call for an appointment. If you call the theaters before the announcement and get put on their waiting list, you will usually be seen even if the theater is a popular one, such as the Cort and the Goodman Theaters.

Some of the Equity theaters audition by invitation only. Hotlines will announce the annual submission deadlines for your P&R.

Since most of the theaters have only one general audition a

year (without per show auditions) you need to give everything you've got. Often outside casting directors and artistic directors are present to view the audition.

## Film and Television

There aren't many film or television productions that originate in Chicago. For those that do come for the locale, the principal casting is done before they reach the city. But there are always extra work and smaller supporting roles left to be cast.

A handful of pilots are set in Chicago each year, most of which don't spawn a series. Yet working on a pilot enables you to be seen on a national level, particularly by casting agents and producers in LA, even if only for one show.

Los Angeles actors will usually win out when it comes to competing for long-term roles. Aspiring television and film actors can get their start in Chicago, but have to make the move to LA if they want to consistently land roles.

Since Chicago is a theater town, television and film actors are considered on the basis of their training rather than their image. If you have a solid skill, you should be seen on the stage and become known by the local casting directors. This can provide a better entré into film and television than heading directly to LA and plunging into the maddening crowd.

## Industrials and Commercials

Since Chicago is a major business center, the corporate market here is extremely good. Most of the union work is AFTRA, but there's also a lot of nonunion production.

Industrials usually don't hire casting directors, so you need to have an agent who specializes in corporate work. Some production companies have an in-house casting staff, and you can contact them directly from the list in *Act One Reports* (see the additional information in the *Publications* section later in this chapter).

Since there is such a large pool of trained theatrical actors, the industrials and commercials in Chicago tend to emphasize character-driven, storytelling types of productions. However, unless you also do stage work, the local snobbery will label you an "industry actor," unfit for serious film or theater work.

In regard to commercials, Chicago rivals New York with the scope of their advertising industry. Many actors find it easy to make a living in Chicago simply by doing commercials or by combining commercials with non-Equity stage work.

The voice-over market is also large, but you must have excellent voice training to compete successfully in Chicago. The fashionable style changes for voice-overs in subtle ways over time, so it's best to have the help of an agent in producing your demo tape.

## Casting

The Chicago theater is considered to be basically male. Women will have better luck getting non-Equity parts, which means they will also have trouble making ends meet by acting only on the stage. There is also more color-blind casting among non-Equity theaters than among those in the Equity.

The Midwestern look (white and All-American) is popular in industrials and commercials, though commercials also tend to hire extremes and unusual character types. Recently, corporations have responded to their diverse work forces and are increasingly hiring actors of different racial and ethnic backgrounds. Bilingual opportunities in the voice-over market are also steadily growing.

## Networking

One of the best ways to network in this city is by performing on the stage, since many agents and casting directors regularly attend the theater. Yet you can find it's possible to make such a good living on stage that you don't even need to pursue commercials or film work.

Networking is often done in a social context in Chicago. The theater and industry parties are a wonderful way to meet people.

Restaurants are also a good way to meet fellow actors as well as producers and directors. Some favorites are

*Sweet Home Chicago*
  ADDRESS: 3270 N. Clark, Chicago, IL 60657
  PHONE: (773) 327-3202

*Joel's Theater Cafe*
  ADDRESS: 3313 N. Clark, Chicago, IL 60657
  PHONE: (773) 871-0896

### *Talent Agents*

Agents are fairly accessible in Chicago, yet getting representation isn't as easy as dropping off your P&R. Research the local agents by using the trade publications and network among fellow actors. Then call the agents who interest you to find out if they have open registrations, which means you can drop off copies of your P&R that they will send to producers and casting agents.

Actors can list with several agencies in Chicago, though many people eventually sign with only one to receive more specialized attention. If you prefer, you can list with several agents for a while in order to discover which one provides the best audition opportunities for you.

In Chicago, agents are typically used for industrials, commercials, television, and film work. Except for stage rules, it's difficult to even get an audition without an agent. But if you want to try, you must have good contact with at least one of the local casting directors.

### *Casting Directors*

Casting directors can be found in *Act One Reports*, and you can call for an appointment to audition. Usually you will be asked to send in your P&R first. Some casting companies specialize in certain areas, such as local commercials, industrials, or extra work.

New York casting directors often come to Chicago looking for talent for commercials, soap operas, and pilots. Los Angeles casting directors come even more regularly seeking new talent, especially for television series, comedies, and movies of the week. It helps to have a good agent who's in touch with the coastal directors, so they can send your videotape to them prior to the pilot season.

## *Talent Unions*

*Actors Equity Association (Equity)*
    MEMBERS: 1,500
    ADDRESS: 203 N. Wabash Ave., 17th Floor, Chicago, IL 60601
    PHONE: (312) 641-0393

*American Federation of Television and Radio Arts* (AFTRA) and *Screen Actor's Guild* (SAG)
    MEMBERS: 2,500
    ADDRESS: 307 N. Michigan Ave., Chicago, IL 60601
    PHONE: (312) 372-8081

## *Professional Associations*

*Bailiwick Repertory Directors Festival*
    ADDRESS: 3212 N. Broadway, Chicago, IL 60657
    PHONE: (312) 883-1091
        This is a festival geared toward directors, yet it is an excellent way to meet a variety of people in the industry. A general audition is held in July.

*Columbia College*, Department of Film and Video
    ADDRESS: 600 S. Michigan, Chicago, IL 60605
    PHONE: (312) 663-1600
        Actors who are interested in participating in student productions can post their name and number on the bulletin board on the eighth floor.

*Music Theater Workshop*
    ADDRESS: 5647 N. Ashland, Chicago, IL 60660
    PHONE: (312) 561-7100
        This organization is an outreach for local teenagers, using actors and performance artists in their productions. You can send your P&R to the Production Coordinator.

## *Publications*

*Act One Reports*
PHONE: (773) 296-4600

This guide is updated three times a year and provides contact information for agents, casting directors, union offices, production companies, advertising agencies, hotlines, and local theaters.

*Acting and Modeling Resource Guide to Chicago*
PHONE: (773) 427-3241

This guide is updated annually and provides lists of instructors, agents, casting directors, and employment agencies.

*Audition News*
ADDRESS: 6272 W. North Ave., Chicago, IL 60639
PHONE: (312) 637-4695

This trade magazine is published monthly and is available by subscription or at local newsstands. It provides lists of agents, casting directors, and theaters, as well as press releases and select auditions.

*Chicago Reader*
ADDRESS: 11 E. Illinois, Chicago, IL 60611
PHONE: (312) 828-0350

This free weekly newspaper is available at retail outlets and streetcorner boxes. It is published on Thursdays and is a source of audition information, particularly in the wanted section of the classifieds.

*Perform Ink*
ADDRESS: 2532 N. Lincoln, Chicago, IL 60614
PHONE: (312) 348-4658

This biweekly publication is available by subscription, and is offered free of charge at agents' offices, theater lobbies, and the Act I Bookstore. It provides general information on the activities of the theater community, occasionally includes audition information, and runs advertisements for teachers and services.

## *Hotlines*

Both Equity and non-Equity hotlines are the best sources of audition information in Chicago.

*Audition News:* (312) 637-2776
> Not as comprehensive as non-Equity, but worth checking.

*Illinois Film Office:* (312) 427-FILM (3456)
> IFO announces calls for extras and stand-ins.

*Non-Equity:* (312) 976-CAST (2278)
> The most comprehensive source of auditions.

## *Talent Books*

*AFTRA/SAG Talent Directory*
ADDRESS/PHONE: See *Talent Unions* above.

## *Talent Showcases*

*Illinois Professional Auditions*
ADDRESS: 1225 W. Belmont Ave, Chicago, IL 60657
PHONE: (312) 929-7288
> This is an annual spring audition held for "students in or completing university degree programs; new-to-Chicago, nonunion actors; and community theater actors."

*Indiana Theater Association*
ADDRESS: 4600 Sunset Ave, Indianapolis, IN 46208
PHONE: (317) 283-9666
> This is an annual audition held in February, usually in Indianapolis (approximately 150 miles south of Chicago). Equity, non-Equity, and experienced student actors may audition.

*League of Chicago Theaters*
ADDRESS: 67 E. Madison, #2116, Chicago, IL 60603
PHONE: (312) 977-1730
> This annual spring audition showcases ethnic, minority, and physically challenged actors, both union and

nonunion. The League also keeps P&Rs on file through the year, making them accessible to local casting directors.

*Michigan Theater Association*
ADDRESS: P.O. Box 726, Marshall, MI 49068
PHONE: (616) 781-7859

This annual audition is held in February, usually in Lansing, MI (approximately 300 miles northeast of Chicago). Though there are some Equity theater apprenticeships available, it is primarily for students and community theater actors.

*National Dinner Theater Association*
ADDRESS: same as the Michigan Theater Association

This annual audition is held in March, in different locations in the central US. They hire primarily non-Equity, and some Equity actors.

## Boston

Boston is an ideal place for the beginning actor to earn a training certificate or a degree in performance arts. The training emphasizes theatrical techniques, and many of the local productions feature established actors from New York.

Boston is the center of the acting industry in New England. Local actors from the populous centers of Connecticut, New Hampshire, Rhode Island, Maine, and Vermont often come to Boston to gain stage experience before trying to tackle New York.

The city of Boston offers a unique mixture of intellectualism, liberal politics, and social conservatism. The pool of actors is relatively small and is considered to be mutually supportive of one another.

Boston is currently suffering from a poor economic situation, constricting some of the acting opportunities in industrial and commercial work that once were readily available.

Actors find that the benefit of living so close to New York is a double-edged sword. They are luckily close enough (approximately 200 miles) to attend auditions and to network among

East Coast casting directors and agents. It is also fairly easy to get the inside scoop on the New York industry from actors who are hired for local productions. Once a Boston actor gets work in New York, then they become desirable assets to the local casting directors. (For more information, also refer to the section of this chapter on New York.)

Most actors use Boston as a launching point for their career because it is difficult to maintain a long-term career there. Theatrical actors require a subsidiary income to work exclusively in the theater. This tightening of the belts has benefited the acting community in terms of camaraderie and the number of creative productions currently happening on the stage.

### Training

Boston is renowned for the quality of its higher education, with several renowned universities in the area. These degree programs offer better-than-average drama courses, occasionally under prominent teachers.

Many of the local theaters also offer training programs and workshops, such as the *New Theater's* two-year program and summer training with *Shakespeare and Co.*

As for private training, there are plenty of teachers and coaches for the beginner, though not as many for serious experienced actors who want to develop their craft.

### Certificate and Degree Programs

*American Repertory Theater*, Institute for Advanced Theater Training at Harvard
    ADDRESS: 64 Brattle St., Cambridge, MA 02138
    PHONE: (617) 495-2668

*Boston Conservatory*
    ADDRESS: 8 The Fenway, Boston, MA 02215
    PHONE: (617) 536-6340

*Boston University*
    ADDRESS: 855 Commonwealth Ave., Boston, MA 02215
    PHONE: (617) 353-3390

Brandeis University, Department of Theater Arts
  ADDRESS: P.O. Box 9110, Waltham, MA 02254
  PHONE: (617) 736-3340

Emerson College
  ADDRESS: 100 Beacon St., Boston, MA 02116
  PHONE: (617) 578-8780

Northeastern University
  ADDRESS: 360 Huntington Ave., Boston, MA 02115
  PHONE: (617) 437-2244

## *Theater*

Regional theaters in Boston, such as The Huntingdon and the American Repertory Theatre (ART), are known for using a great deal of outside talent, primarily from New York. The American Repertory Theater also typically casts actors from the ART Institute at Harvard.

The Merrimack draws heavily on local talent for their productions and operates under LORT contracts. Other local Equity theaters operate under COST and SPT contracts, and while LOAs don't pay as much, they can offer long-running opportunities for local actors (see chapter 3 for more details).

There are a number of non-Equity theaters in Boston. Some do not produce shows often, while others have respected companies that generate regular work. However the pay is low, sometimes merely a stipend. There are also a large number of community theaters where non-Equity professionals and less experienced new actors can build their resumés and expand their skills.

### Auditions

Most of the local theaters hold annual auditions and send representatives to the *StageSource* auditions (see *Professional Associations* below). Actors can also contact theaters directly, send your P&R and call to ask about an appointment to audition.

Open auditions are rare, and callbacks often last half a day or

more, with casting directors pairing different actors to get a feel
for the available combinations.

### Film and Television

The Massachusetts Film Office is the agency which fosters
movie production in the area. Currently, local television stations (both PBS and commercial) are the most regular producers of dramatic shows that are cast locally. Cable stations
also provide opportunities for employment.

Boston has been the home of several national long-running
TV series (such as *Spenser for Hire* and *Against the Law*). It is
also regularly the site of feature films and productions for
*American Playhouse,* as well as independent and student films
from the numerous universities and performance art institutes
in the area.

### Industrials and Commercials

The Boston area has been hit hard by the economic recession
in New England, and production and advertising budgets have
been severely cut. Yet the local AFTRA/SAG office reports that
most of their members' earnings during the early '90s came
from industrials.

Many of the national industrials come to Boston for the
locale, yet their casting is often done in New York. In order to
make a living, it helps if you can model or do print work (still
photographs for advertising). The voice-over market is also
quite strong.

Commercial production is mainly limited to local spots. In
the few national productions, the principals are usually cast in
New York or Los Angeles.

### Casting

A number of nontraditional and minority casting oppor-
tunities exit in Boston theater, there are the Black Folks'
Theater, The Company of Women, Playwrights' Platform, and
Wheelock Family Theater. In Boston, ethnic and minority

actors will work more in industrials than any other area and, in general, have a difficult time being cast.

Most industrial productions are looking for actors who fit their vision of corporate CEO-types, thirtysomething managers, and young business graduates. This market, as well as the voice-over market, is predominantly male.

### Networking

Boston is a small city when it comes to square miles, and the community is friendly enough to make networking a fundamental part of your success.

Many of the theater companies, particularly Playwrights' Platform, sponsor readings of new plays. According to the local actors, joining the professional association, StageSource, and participating in their events and classes is the best way to get to know theater professionals and find jobs.

### Talent Agents

Despite the local preference for union productions, the recession helped opened the market to nonunion activity, particularly in industrials and commercials. The budgets for non-union industry productions are usually low enough that non-franchised agents and production houses are used rather than independent casting directors.

Only one-tenth of the talent agents and casting directors in the Boston area are franchised by AFTRA/SAG. These agencies typically represent both modeling and acting work.

Many actors work in Boston without being listed with any agent at all, while others find it is useful to be listed with one or more of the franchised and non-franchised agents. Agents can often provide work for lower budget film and broadcast projects that don't employ casting directors.

### Casting Directors

Casting directors hold much of the employment power in Boston. Independent casting directors work for corporate clients as well as production houses. Local stages usually handle their own casting, but if they're busy or having trouble with a particular role, they will turn to casting directors.

There are about ten casting companies in the Boston area, but only a few get the bulk of the work: Colling/Pickman and Outcasting are two of the better-known companies. Outcasting is currently holding biannual auditions.

### Talent Unions

Boston has always been known as a union town no matter what trade you're in. If you are interested in work in the theater, film, or television, it's practically necessary for you to join one of the local unions.

*Actors Equity Association* (Equity), Liaison City
MEMBERS: 550
ADDRESS/PHONE: see the section on talent unions under New York

*American Federation of Television and Radio Artists* (AFTRA)
MEMBERS: 1,524
ADDRESS: 11 Beacon St., #512, Boston, MA 02108
PHONE: (617) 742-2688

*Screen Actors' Guild* (SAG)
MEMBERS: 900
ADDRESS/PHONE: see the section on talent unions under New York

### Professional Associations

*StageSource*
ADDRESS: 1 Boylston Place, Boston, MA 02116
PHONE: (617) 423-2475

StageSource was founded in 1985 as an arts advocacy, resource, and service organization for actors and other theater professionals. Membership dues are annual and services include a casting hotline, Talent Book, and workshops. They also publish *The Source*. (See below for more information on talent books and talent showcases in the Boston area.)

## Cultural Education Collaborative
ADDRESS: 201 South St., Boston, MA 02111
PHONE: (617) 338-3073

The CEC promotes "the cultural education of Massachusetts' diverse student populations" through work with performers, mimes, puppeteers, and dancers. Artists work with and/or present to other students.

## First Night Arts Celebration
ADDRESS: P.O. Box 573, Back Bay Annex, Boston, MA 02117
PHONE: (617) 542-1399

This celebration takes place every year from December 29–31 and includes performing arts, video, and visual arts presented in various locations. Participants include performance artists, storytellers, musical groups, and many more. Call to receive an application.

## International Television Association (ITVA)
ADDRESS: 26 Constitution Drive, Southborough, MA 01772
PHONE: (617) 890-4882

The International Television Association offers workshops and meetings for producers, directors, and talent interested in the field of television.

## New England Producers Association (NEPA)
ADDRESS: 1380 Soldiers Field Rd., Boston, MA 02135
PHONE: (617) 698-6372

Many local actors belong to NEPA in order to meet producers and directors. Their newsletter, *The Slate*, has a column called "Actor's Corner" and advertises actor-director workshops that allow members of the industry to network. Workshops are open to both NEPA members and nonmembers, and are announced on the AFTRA/SAG and StageSource hotlines.

*The Open Door Theater Company*
ADDRESS: P.O. Box 315, Jamaica Plain, MA 02130
PHONE: (617) 524-4007

    This is an outdoor theater company that performs in a local city park. Casting is done by audition each year and open to non-Equity only.

*Playwrights' Platform*
ADDRESS: 164 Brayton Rd., Boston, MA 02130
PHONE: (617) 254-4482

    This is a "developmental theater for new plays" and members include actors, playwrights, and directors. They hold Sunday readings where you can network, as well as monthly Playwrights' Brunches. Both Equity and non-Equity actors participate in the readings.

*Revels, Inc.*
ADDRESS: 1 Kendall Square, Building 600, Cambridge, MA 02139
PHONE: (617) 621-0505

    Biannually, in the spring and winter, the Revels present a seasonal celebration combining drama, song, and dance. Auditions are held for a volunteer chorus of both professionals and non-professionals.

*Theatre in Process*
ADDRESS: 220 Marlborough St., Boston, MA 02116
PHONE: (617) 267-1053

    Theater in Process develops scripts, primarily for the Wheelock Family Theater, from readings to full production. P&Rs are accepted from both Equity and non-Equity actors.

## Publications

*Boston Phoenix*
ADDRESS: 126 Brookline Ave., Boston, MA 02134
PHONE: (617) 536-5390

    This is a big weekly alternative newspaper published

on Fridays. It lists most of the audition notices. It is available at any newsstand.

*Casting News*
ADDRESS: P.O. Box 201, Boston, MA 02134
PHONE: (617) 787-2991

A bimonthly publication, the *News* is available by subscription or at major newsstands in both Boston and Cambridge. It includes acting and musical auditions, resources and events information, play competitions, funding information, and articles.

*New England Entertainment Digest* (NEED)
ADDRESS: P.O. Box 313, Portland, CT 06480
PHONE: (203) 342-4730

A monthly publication, NEED is available by subscription or at major Boston newsstands. It includes an events calendar, press releases, entertainment news, and reviews. The audition notices are usually for community theater, but the press releases (announcing a movie production coming to the area for example) are applicable to professional actors.

## Talent Books

*AFTRA/SAG Talent Guide*
ADDRESS/PHONE: see the talent unions section above

This guide is published every three years for members only. A midterm supplement updates information and adds the names of new members.

*StageSource*
ADDRESS/PHONE: see the publications section above

When you join StageSource you are allowed to place your P&R in three categories and, for a small annual fee, you may choose additional categories. StageSource also maintains an Equal Opportunity P&R file for ethnic and minority actors and actors with disabilities, which is open to both members and non-members.

*Talent Showcases*

*New England Theater Conference* (NETC)
ADDRESS: 50 Exchange St., Waltham, MA 02154
PHONE: (617) 893-3120

This annual Showcase is held every March at different locations in the Boston area. Most producers and casting directors are from non-Equity summer stock theaters, but some from year-round theaters attend as well.

*StageSource*
ADDRESS/PHONE: see the publications section above

This annual combined audition is announced six weeks in advance. The Equity audition is open to all eligible actors; the non-Equity auditions are for Stage-Source members only. Audition slots are filled on a first-come, first-serve basis. These auditions are primarily attended by local casting directors and producers.

## Washington, D.C.

The capital of our nation is a distinct entity unto itself. Washington, D.C. includes the neighboring city-suburbs in Maryland and Virginia. The nearby city of Baltimore has been the home of several large film productions, with Barry Levinson returning to shoot *Rain Man, Diner, Avalon,* and the TV series *Homicide.*

Washington, D.C. is a favorite for its locale. It has European charm in its old neighborhoods and urban excitement in its business centers. The monuments are key for certain film productions, and the many transient and international residents lend a bustling quality to the city.

Like Boston, D.C. is approximately four hours away from New York, which means working actors are close enough to attend auditions or interviews. Washington, D.C. can also be used as a stepping stone to reach the professional levels of work in New York.

While Boston is better for theater actors, D.C. is ideal for actors who can work in industrials. Washington, D.C. is a government town, and various federal agencies produce countless industrial training films. Though industrial work doesn't lead to stardom, it is an excellent way for an actor to make a living while pursuing other work.

The Screen Actors' Guild's report in the early '90s stated that D.C. had the fastest growing earnings market, but then it had nowhere to go but up. Producers and directors of films and television, in D.C. usually bring in talent from New York or Los Angeles. Local actors don't hesitate to say that many of the principal Equity jobs for both men and women aren't cast locally.

Though D.C. is not considered a major theater center, it has a strong, supportive community. Over forty theaters in the area participate in the Helen Hayes Awards, developed to increase awareness of theater in D.C. Actors find that it is possible to make a living on the stage, but do not expect to leap to national fame by performing in D.C.

Washington, D.C. offers a more suburban lifestyle for working actors (with affordable housing in outlying suburbs like Takoma Park). The climate is moderate, with a few cold winter months a year and some snowfall. The spring and summer are beautiful in D.C., though some days are hot and humid.

### Training

There are a variety of training options in D.C., from universities to theater workshops and even a few excellent private coaches.

The unions are very supportive, offering a workshop each month, while the Actors' Center organizes free Saturday-morning workshops. Theaters have well-respected programs, such as The Shakespeare Theater's three month workshop for college interns and the three-month saturday program that fits the working professional's schedule.

*Certificate and Degree Programs*

*American University*, Department of Performing Arts
   ADDRESS: 4400 Massachusetts Ave., NW, Washington, D.C. 20016
   PHONE: (202) 885-3420

*Howard University*, Department of Theater Arts
  ADDRESS: 6th and Fairmount St., NW, Washington, D.C.
  20059
  PHONE: (202) 806-7050

*University of Maryland/Baltimore County*, Theater
Department
  ADDRESS: 5401 Wilkens Ave., Baltimore, MD 21228
  PHONE: (301) 455-2949

## *Theater*

Washington, D.C. is the home of several world-famous theaters, such as the National Theater, Kennedy Center, and Ford's
Theater. There are also many well-respected regional companies such as the Arena Stage and The Shakespeare Theater.
The mix of actors on the local stage is remarkable—The
Shakespeare Theater frequently brings in stars for its productions, yet for smaller roles and understudy parts students and
apprentices from the training programs are used. The Kennedy
Center does some of its own producing as well as presenting
outside shows.

The League of Washington Theaters has helped create a vital
community of both small and large theaters. Community
theater is also strong, as is dinner and musical theater. Since
D.C. is such a conservative town, there isn't much experimental
theater (though notable exceptions are the Woolly Mammoth
and Scena).

Though most actors get paid, very few are contracted on a
full-time, salaried basis. Non-Equity actors can work at both
the nonunion and the large numbers of SPT theaters. Equity
actors are able to work under Guest Artist Contracts and Letters
of Agreement.

Actors should send their P&Rs to local theaters (get a list
from the Equity office) and actively pursue an appointment to
audition. They should also participate in talent showcases and
general auditions, since most of the local casting personnel

attend. Occasionally theaters still hold open calls, especially when there's difficulty casting a role.

### Film and Television

Though the locale is unmistakable (or perhaps because of it) there is little film on television work in D.C. Yet the region (from Maryland down to Richmond, VA) does get at least half a dozen productions each year. There are usually also a few TV pilots, some PBS programming, and a few non-union dramas from local cable stations. Producers use local casting agencies to hire everything from bit players and extras to principal cast members.

### Industrials and Commercials

The Screen Actors' Guild reports that the D.C. area is among the handful of cities in the nation reporting very high earnings for industrials and commercials. This is primarily because the US government hires a lot of talent to do industrials for departments such as the US Postal Service, the IRS, the EPA, and many more. Some government agencies even have their own production houses, as do the numerous corporations and lobbyists in the area.

Though there is a non-union market for commercials, most of the work is done through SAG. The union can give you a list of the local production houses which you can contact directly to submit your P&R.

Commercial productions tend to take place in Baltimore, while industrials are centered in D.C., but basically these two cities form one giant, sprawling acting community.

### Casting

Keep in mind that the city is conservative, so many of the production companies aren't interested in pushing the limits. Casting for the largest market—industrials and commercials— tends to go with conservative, clean-cut corporate types, though they also need younger narrators and spokespeople.

Most of the roles require actors of the All-American type who can play middle-class family members, as well as thirty-something blue collar types.

There is practically no need for non-traditional talent when it comes to these industrials, and you'll do little better in the commercial market. However, older talent is sought after for commercials, including those with an upper-income look.

Many theaters are better about casting against type, and you'll find more ethnic and minority roles than there were ten years ago. The Shakespeare Theater is consistent about their color-blind casting (they have a liaison program with Howard University). There is also a growing demand for bilingual actors, primarily Asian and Hispanic.

### Networking

The best places to network are the Actors' Center and the Backstage Bookstore. The only performing arts bookstore in the area, Backstage carries a full line of scripts, tapes, and periodicals, and posts casting notices.

Backstage Books
ADDRESS: 2101 P St., NW, Washington, D.C. 20037
PHONE: (202) 775-1488

Auditions and talent showcases are much more popular places to network than restaurants, but there are a few that are favorites of actors.

Dante's
ADDRESS: 1522 14th St., NW, Washington, D.C. 20036
PHONE: (202) 677-7260

Herb's
ADDRESS: 1615 Rhode Island Ave., NW, Washington, D.C. 20036
PHONE: (202) 333-4372

### Talent Agents and Casting Directors

In D.C., there isn't much difference between talent agents

and casting directors. Very few of the agencies are affiliated with AFTRA and SAG, and almost none are involved in theater.

Some call themselves "casting agencies," a combination of an agent and a casting company. With training and a little experience, it should be easy to find representation among casting companies, especially for union members. Exclusive contracts are rare, and most actors are registered with several agencies.

Since the acting community is fairly small, the casting companies are always looking for new faces. Yet it's not enough to have your P&R on file; you have to actively network among the local casting directors. You can find a list of the local agencies from Actors' Center or AFTRA/SAG.

### Talent Unions

*Actors' Equity Association* (Equity) Liaison City
MEMBERS: 500 (Washington, D.C. and Baltimore)
ADDRESS: see the section on talent unions under New York

*American Federation of Television and Radio Artists* (AFTRA)
MEMBERS: 2,700
ADDRESS: 5480 Wisconsin Ave, #201, Chevy Chase, MD 20815
PHONE: (301) 657-2560

*Screen Actors' Guild* (SAG)
MEMBERS: 1,200
ADDRESS/PHONE: same as AFTRA

### Professional Associations

*Actors' Center*
ADDRESS: P.O. Box 50180, Washington, D.C. 20091
PHONE: (202) 638-3777

This organization provides a bimonthly newsletter (*On Cue!*), an audition hotline, and an annual talent showcase.

It also holds workshops every Saturday morning on everything from theatrical makeup to musical auditioning.

*Washington Theater Festival*
ADDRESS: 1835 14th St., NW, Washington, D.C. 20009
PHONE: (202) 462-1073
   The Source Theater produces an annual summer fes-
tival of new plays, held in a variety of locations. Auditions
are held in June.

## Publications

*City Paper*
   This weekly publication comes out on Thursdays and is
freely distributed around the city. It has a few audition
notices, mostly for community theater and workshops.

*Washington Post*
   Theaters run audition notices in the Friday edition's
weekend section and sometimes in the Sunday edition.

## Talent Books

*The Actors' Center*
ADDRESS/PHONE: see *Professional Organizations* above
   This organization maintains a P&R file of all its members and makes it available to local casting directors and
agencies.

*League of Washington Theaters*
ADDRESS: 410 8th St., NW, Suite 600, Washington, D.C.
20004
PHONE: (202) 638-4270
   The League maintains an extensive talent file. Any
actor can send in his or her P&R to be included.

*Producers' Audition Hotline*
ADDRESS: P.O. Box 742, Olney, MD 20830
PHONE: (301) 924-5700
   This talent bank is for voice-over talent. You can pay to

include your demo, which is heard by producers, casting directors, and others throughout the Northeast.

## Talent Showcases

*The Actors' Center*
ADDRESS/PHONE: see *the professional organizations* section above

The February auditions and the December Scene Showcase are open to participation by members of the Actors' Center. Slots for the auditions are filled by lottery, and you must audition to be included in the Showcase. Call for more information.

*American Federation of Television and Radio Artists/Screen Actors' Guild*
ADDRESS/PHONE: see talent unions section above

Recently, the talent unions have begun holding an annual talent showcase. You must audition to be included, and participants present scenes, monologues, or songs to producers, casting directors, and directors.

*League of Washington Theaters*
ADDRESS/PHONE: see the talent books section above

The League holds an annual, week-long audition during the summer. It is open to all actors who can supply enough P&Rs to distribute to attending producers, casting personnel, and directors. The audition is announced in the Washington Post and on the Actors' Center Hotline.

# Philadelphia

Philadelphia is the home of the first community theater, and the oldest continually-used theater in the US, the Walnut Street Theater. It also has one of the first drama colleges, the Philadelphia College of Performing Arts.

There is an ethnic and cultural diversity in and around Philadelphia with a strong working-class ethic. Yet this city has also suffered financially in recent years, and artistic endeavors have been greatly affected. Various directors and agents have been meeting for the past few years in order to create a viable theater community under the name of the Performing Arts League.

In order to find enough work, many actors must travel to New York or Washington, D.C. to audition (both cities are only a couple hours away by train). Actors who are working in industrials in Philadelphia and D.C. and are actively pursuing television work in New York sometimes choose to live in Philadelphia to split their travel time and cut down living expenses.

Philadelphia is also a good location for actors who don't want to commit to a full-time acting career. Talented actors can be seen and noticed in this small community, and there is the added benefit of rubbing shoulders with the nearby New York casting directors and producers, which may bring lucrative opportunities.

It's easy to find affordable housing in Philadelphia, whether it's in Center City or the surrounding suburbs. The climate is wet year-round and fairly moderate, though the muggy heat in the summer can sometimes be oppressive.

### Training

Many of the local theater companies offer classes, yet most of the professional actors in the area commute to New York for additional training. The best teachers can be found at the Wilma Theater and at The Actors' Center, which teaches on-camera skills.

#### Certificate and Degree Programs

*University of the Arts,* Philadelphia College of Performing Arts
  ADDRESS: 313 S. Broad St., Philadelphia, PA 19102
  PHONE: (215) 875-2232

*Villanova University*, Theater Department
ADDRESS: 108 Vasey Hall, Villanova, PA 19085
PHONE: (215) 645-7545

## *Theater*

Though Philadelphia once was a main stop on the way to Broadway for most large productions, those days are long gone. Since the late '80s, however, Philadelphia has been compared to Chicago in light of its burgeoning community theater scene and the many premieres of new plays scheduled each year.

The theaters usually hold local auditions, but many of the casting directors turn to New York as a matter of course. And there's the added problem of New York actors commuting down to Philadelphia for the auditions.

Yet Drama Guild, a prominent local theater, does much of its casting locally. In Philadelphia, it doesn't matter if you are hired by a large theater or community theater; most actors get paid. And dinner theaters are a booming business in the surrounding suburbs.

Most theaters have general auditions once a year. These aren't usually announced, so you will have to call to find out how to sign up.

## *Film and Television*

Features are occasionally shot in Philadelphia to take advantage of its particular atmosphere (*Rocky* and its sequels, for example). When a production does come to Philadelphia, many of the local Equity actors are put to use as extras and bit players. Unfortunately, this doesn't happen as often as anyone would like.

There aren't any TV series based in Philadelphia, and even the most memorable one set there, *thirtysomething* was shot in LA. Occasionally the local PBS station does produce dramatic shows.

## *Industrials and Commercials*

There is a fairly strong corporate market in and around Philadelphia. The work is mostly non-union. To find jobs, you must make contact with the local casting directors, though some of the production houses accept P&Rs directly from actors.

Both union and non-union actors can find work in commercials. But again many casting directors head to New York to find new faces since the talent pool is rather small in the Philadelphia area.

### Casting

Younger Equity actors, particularly women, may have trouble getting work in Philadelphia. Commercials cast actors with a typical corporate look to play sales representatives, executives, and middle-class families. The most work goes to people in the thirty-five-to-fifty age range, particularly male corporate types in their forties. But in the theater, non-traditional casting is undergoing a revival, and actors of many races and ethnicities are being more frequently utilized. Minority actors are also getting more work in the commercial and industrial market.

### Networking

Networking can be of real benefit to you in the Philadelphia area since some theaters actually send casting notices to actors who have previously worked for them. Some even send notices to actors who have auditioned for them.

The city is small enough that you can do most of your networking at auditions and play readings. There are also popular bars and restaurants near the theaters.

Moriarty's
ADDRESS: 1116 Walnut St., Philadelphia, PA 19107
PHONE: (215) 627-7676

16th Street Bar and Grill
ADDRESS: 264 S. 16th St., Philadelphia, PA 19102
PHONE: (215) 735-3316

### Talent Agents and Casting Directors

There are only a few talent agents and casting directors in

Philadelphia, serving mainly print, film, and industrial work. Agents are also good for referring actors to auditions in other Northeastern cities, such as Baltimore, Pittsburgh, and sometimes even New York.

Getting listed with an agency isn't too difficult if you have training and/or experience. Even if you do sign with an agent, it usually won't be exclusive.

Pursuing an agent or casting director isn't necessary to work on the stage since you can contact the theaters directly.

### Talent Unions

*Actors' Equity Association* (Equity), Liaison City
MEMBERS: 400
ADDRESS/PHONE: see the section talent unions under New York

*American Federation of Television and Radio Artists* (AFTRA)
MEMBERS: 1,700
ADDRESS: 230 S. Broad St., 10th Floor, Philadelphia, PA 19102
PHONE: (215) 732-0507

*Screen Actors' Guild* (SAG)
MEMBERS: 900
ADDRESS: 230 S. Broad St., 10th Floor, Philadelphia, PA 19102
PHONE: (215) 545-3150

### Professional Associations

*Bushfire Theater's 52nd Street Writers Workshop*
ADDRESS: 224 S. 52nd St., Philadelphia, PA 19139
PHONE: (215) 747-9230

This workshop holds twice-weekly readings. Most of these readings are cast with actors who have appeared in the Bushfire Theater, but others are called for auditions from their P&Rs. Call for schedules and an audition appointment.

*Play Works*
ADDRESS: 623 South St., Philadelphia, PA 19147
PHONE: (215) 592-8393

This organization is dedicated to developing new projects, including staged readings and community outreach. Auditions are held twice a year, and are announced in *Stage.*

*The Royal Pickwickians*
ADDRESS: 2008 Mt. Vernon St., Philadelphia, PA 19130
PHONE: (215) 232-2690

This organization specializes in historical interpretation, producing murder mysteries, theme-based parties, and event entertainment for school programs, museums, and the Historical Society of Pennsylvania. Non-Equity actors may submit their P&R.

## Publications

*The Actor's Casting Guide*
This directory is the first place to turn when you're looking for casting resources in the Philadelphia area.

*Stage: A Theater Monthly*
ADDRESS: 9 E. Rose Valley Rd., Wallingford, PA 19066
PHONE: (215) 565-2094

This monthly publication is available by subscription and is distributed free to theaters and schools. It provides audition notices for mostly non-Equity work, production listings, and advertisements for classes and services.

## Talent Books

*American Federation of Television and Radio Artists/Screen Actors' Guild*
ADDRESS/PHONE: see the talent unions section above

The Philadelphia Talent Guide is published every three years and is only for members of AFTRA/SAG.

## *Talent Showcases*

*Performing Arts League of Philadelphia*
ADDRESS: c/o The Wilma Theater, 2030 Sansom St., Philadelphia, PA 19103
PHONE: (215) 963-0249
This association of professional companies and organizations sponsors an annual audition that is attended by member theaters. Auditions are announced in *Stage*.

# San Francisco

As far as the acting industry is concerned, San Francisco is like the West Coast equivalent of Boston. San Franciso is a cultural city, albeit a more experimental one for learning and the arts, and the emphasis is on theatrical training and stage work. Just as Boston actors look to New York for work and advancement in film and television, most actors in San Francisco look to Los Angeles to find consistent work, although at twice the distance. This somewhat isolates the San Francisco acting community and there is less overlap between the West Coast acting pools than you find in East Coast cities, which are connected by the rail system.

San Francisco is known for its experimental theater and special ensemble groups. Though the work may not be as widely seen as in Los Angeles, the productions are usually very high-quality and it's not impossible to be "discovered" by casting directors and producers from the bigger market to the south. Bay Area actors are well-respected in LA, and there is a steady stream of talent moving south after having earned their credentials. The soaps, in particular, often conduct talent searches in San Francisco.

In San Francisco, as in Chicago, the quality of your training is considered to be an important part of your reputation. The theater community tends to be a bit snobbish, with less crossover between it and the commercial and industrial markets.

The Bay Area is huge, encompassing San Francisco and nine other counties, including the cities of Berkeley and Oakland. Unfortunately, the Bay Area is also one of the most expensive places to live in the country. The climate is cool and often foggy, with milder, dryer summers.

### *Training*

Good training is readily available in the Bay Area, whether it's through university programs, theater institutes, or private schools. Acting techniques are an extensive part of training, as are on-camera and auditioning skills.

The programs at the renowned American Conservatory Theater include the Young Conservatory, the Academy, and the Summer Training Congress, which attract students from across the nation. Also renowned is the Jean Shelton Actors Lab, which has been operating in the area for over twenty years.

Theaters such as the Marin Theater Company and the Eureka offer workshops, while private schools are listed in *Callboard*, the monthly publication of the professional organization Theater Bay Area (see the publications section below).

*Certificate and Degree Programs*

*American Conservatory Theater*
   ADDRESS: 450 Geary St., San Francisco, CA 94102
   PHONE: (415) 749-2350

*City College of San Francisco*, Drama Department
   ADDRESS: 50 Phelan Ave., San Francisco, CA 94112
   PHONE: (415) 239-3132

*San Francisco State University*, Department of Theater Arts
   ADDRESS: 1600 Holloway Ave., San Francisco, CA 94132
   PHONE: (415) 338-1341

*University of California*, Berkeley, Dramatic Art Department
   ADDRESS: 101 Dwinelle Annex, Berkeley, CA 94720
   PHONE: (510) 642-1677

## Theater

San Francisco was well known for its experimental theater during the '60s and '70s, particularly during the development of Sam Shepard's plays, the San Francisco Mime Troupe, and the American Conservatory Theater and local critics still seem to favor experimental productions over traditional ones.

The top LORT theaters are ACT and the Berkeley Repertory Theater. ACT tends to cast out of town or through their own training program, as do the California Shakespeare Festival, the San Francisco Shakespeare Festival, and the San Jose Repertory Company. The local per-show auditions are usually on an invitation-only basis, and monologues are preferred.

The Eureka Theater, the Magic Theater, and companies such as the San Jose Stage Company and the Marin Shakespeare Festival are covered by Equity's Bay Area Theater Contract. These theaters occasionally hold open calls, and even noneligible actors can ask to be seen if there is time. If you can't get a slot, go on the day of the audition and ask to be put on a waiting list.

It's not easy to get your Equity card in San Francisco, but there are plenty of non-Equity local theaters where you can be seen and gain valuable experience. Non-Equity actors can be hired in Equity theaters under Guest Artist contracts and the Bay Area Project Policy.

There is also a thriving community of constituent-specific theaters such as the African-American Shakespeare Festival, Asian-American Theater Company, Theatre del'Esperanza, and the Theater of Yugen.

## Film and Television

San Francisco has one of the best-organized AFTRA/SAG offices in the country, with an active hotline that constantly apprises actors of work. The local PBS station, KQED, occasionally produces dramatic programming, and pilots and features are often shot in San Francisco to take advantage of the striking locale.

Talent agents tend to look to the theater to find new actors for the screen. Many of the agents have ties to Los Angeles, and regularly send videotapes of their clients downstate during pilot season. San Francisco is also a stop on the national searches performed by film companies and the soaps.

Yet despite the support, it's nearly impossible to maintain a film and television career in San Francisco. If that's your goal, you will have to make the move four hundred miles south to LA at some point to land principal roles.

### Industrials and Commercials

There are a number of corporations based in the Bay Area and though the recession has hit Silicon Valley rather hard, there is still plenty of work for local actors. Many people find they can support themselves doing industrials and commercials, but the actors who are trying to establish a screen or stage career don't usually talk about their industrial work.

Most of the industrials are produced under the union. It's essential to have a good agent who specializes in industrials since most companies bypass casting directors.

The Bay Area is a favorite test market for commercials, so many are produced locally. There is also a growing trend to produce infommercials here.

### Networking

As in the other technique-oriented cities, networking in San Francisco is done more often in classes than in restaurants or local hangouuts. Many actors in San Francisco participate in classes and do volunteer work at local festivals and educational programs.

However, the best networking can be done at the Theater Bay Area whose auditions are an essential way to be seen.

### Talent Agents and Casting Directors

In the past ten years, there has been a blossoming of both talent agents and casting directors in the Bay Area. Most are union franchised, by Equity, SAG, or AFTRA.

Networking is the best way to find out which agent is right

for you. You won't have to sign an exclusive contract so you can try out a few agents until you find the one who represents you best. In order to get strong representation, you will eventually have to go exclusive. Agents rarely handle theater, except for some of the touring shows. But for film and corporate work, you will definitely need an agent.

Even agented actors can send their P&R to casting directors for their files, and follow up with notices of current work. The Nancy Hayes Casting company handles quite a bit of the extra and principal casting in the area. Actors can bring their P&R and register with her office on any weekday afternoon.

## Talent Unions

Actors' Equity Association (Equity)
MEMBERS: 800
ADDRESS: 235 Pine St., San Francisco, CA 94104
PHONE: (415) 391-3838

American Federation of Television and Radio Artists (AFTRA)
MEMBERS: 2,700
ADDRESS: same as Equity
PHONE: (415) 391-7510

Screen Actors' Guild (SAG)
MEMBERS: 2,200
ADDRESS/PHONE: same as Equity

## Professional Associations

Theater Bay Area
ADDRESS: 657 Mission St., #402, San Francisco, CA 94105
PHONE: (415) 957-1557

This organization is a resource and communications network for the performing arts community. Services include group health insurance, a talent book, annual combined auditions, and casting information. Theater Bay Area publishes Callboard, Theater Directory, and Sources of Publicity.

*Performing Arts Workshop*
ADDRESS: Fort Mason Center, Building C, #265, San Francisco, CA 94123
PHONE: (415) 673-2634

This not-for-profit organization works with several local programs, including Artists in Schools and Theater for Elders. Salaried nonunion jobs are announced in *Callboard*, *Dance Bay Area*, and the *Bay Guardian*, or send a P&R with cover letter for an appointment to audition.

*Playwrights' Center of San Francisco*
ADDRESS: 3225 Laguna St., #3, San Francisco, CA 94123
PHONE: (415) 763-2727

The Center sponsors readings and an annual play contest. Auditions are held twice yearly and the group meets every Friday night. Actors interested in developing and producing new stage works may attend and bring their P&R.

*The Playwrights' Foundation*
ADDRESS: P.O. Box 460357, San Francisco, CA 94146
PHONE: (415) 777-2996

This annual summer festival consists of new play readings and productions. Auditions are announced in *Callboard* and on the Equity hotline.

*Student Film*, San Francisco State University Department of Cinema
ADDRESS: Attn. Actors Book, 1600 Holloway Ave., San Francisco, CA 94132
PHONE: (415) 338-2466

Actors may send their P&R for inclusion in this book if they want to volunteer for student filmmakers at SFSU.

## Publications

*Callboard*
ADDRESS/PHONE: see professional organizations section above

This monthly publication is published by Theater Bay Area and is available by subscription (included in the TBA membership) or at newsstands and bookstores. It includes audition notices, articles, theater listings, and advertisements for services and workshops.

*San Francisco Chronicle*
ADDRESS: 925 Mission, San Francisco, CA 94103
PHONE: (415) 777-7000
This morning newspaper occasionally carries audition notices in the classifieds. They also provide some information on current local productions.

## Hotlines and Bulletin Boards

*American Conservatory Theater*
ADDRESS: 450 Geary St., San Francisco, CA 94102
The ACT's fourth floor bulletin board posts local and out-of-town auditions. Anyone can enter and review the notices.

*Nancy Hayes Casting: (415) 567-0108*
This casting company primarily lists calls for nonunion extra work.

*Theater Bay Area Member Hotline: (415) 957-1557*
This hotline is only for members of TBA.

## Talent Books

*Theater Bay Area*
ADDRESS/PHONE: see the professional organizations section above
This talent book contains listings of members of TBA.

## Talent Showcases

*American Federation of Television and Radio Artists/Screen Actors' Guild Equal Opportunity Showcase*
ADDRESS/PHONE: see the talent unions section above
The unions' Equal Employment Opportunity Commit-

tee presents a showcase two or three times a year that offers local members the chance to show themselves in nonstereotypical roles to producers, casting personnel, and directors. Showcases are announced on the AFTRA/ SAG hotline and in union newsletters.

*Theater Bay Area*
ADDRESS/PHONE: see the professional organizations section above

The Theater Bay Area holds annual auditions that are attended by casting personnel and directors from Bay Area theaters. All actors may participate, including Equity and experienced nonunion TBA members. Auditions are announced in *Callboard.*

## Seattle

During the '90s, Seattle became the new mecca for actors tired of trying to make it in the big cities. But so many people were lured to Seattle by the quality-of-living reports of plenty of accessible nature, good schools, good karma, and low costs that some people say this city has become over-full of aspiring actors.

Theater is big in Seattle, with some of the Equity theaters creating productions that go all the way to Broadway. Just as grunge-rock came out of this area in the late '80s, the acting community also considered itself on the forefront of experimental acting. If you're a poor, trained actor who is interested in pushing the limits of your craft, the Northwest could be perfect for you.

### *Training*

Most actors tend to come to Seattle having already trained elsewhere. There's plenty of additional training for the inexperienced actor, but for the film and television actor there aren't many opportunities for honing your skills except for casting directors who teach on-camera skills. The *Handbook* (see the publications section below) can give you names of some quality workshops and classes.

## Certificate and Degree Programs

Cornish College of the Arts
  ADDRESS: 710 E. Roy St., Seattle, WA 98102
  PHONE: (206) 323-1400, ext. 320

University of Washington, School of Drama
  ADDRESS: DX-20, Seattle, WA 98195
  PHONE: (206) 543-5140

## Theater

Seattle may be a young theater town, but it has already gained national renown with its boom in quality productions and influx of actors. Portland (150 miles south) is considered to be the up-and-coming center for fringe theater.

The Seattle-Tacoma area has over a dozen Equity theaters, and there have even been a few major Broadway shows that were developed at the Seattle Repertory Theater. The primary LORT theaters are A Contemporary Theater (ACT), Intiman Theater, and Seattle Rep. Letter of Agreement companies include Bellevue Repertory Theater, Center Stage, the Empty Space, Seattle Group Theater, and Seattle Shakespeare Festival.

The union theaters tend to cast out of town, but the general auditions are a great way to be seen. The regional Equity union (REACT) sponsors auditions that are attended by casting directors from regional theaters around the country.

The majority of theaters in the Seattle area are considered "fringe"—non-Equity companies that produce new and exciting productions. Some of these use Guest Artist contracts or LOAs for their Equity performers. Auditions are announced on the League of Fringe Theaters (LOFT) hotline.

## Film and Television

The Northwest has gotten a big shot in the arm with productions such as *Twin Peaks* and *Northern Exposure*. In any large production, the principals are cast before they arrive on location, yet there is a lot of work for day players and extras.

Local agents try to maintain contacts with Los Angeles, sending their actors' videotapes down during pilot season. There are also a few national searches for soaps every year. But, needless to say, it's difficult to make a living in film and television in the Northwest.

## *Industrials and Commercials*

There are enough industrials produced in the area to make it a viable field of work (the productions are split between union and non-union). Boeing is only one of the large corporations in the area that is quite productive when it comes to shooting industrials.

Some production houses hire casting directors while others go straight to the agents. Actors can also find the names and addresses of houses which accept P&Rs directly.

Both local and national commercial production keeps local actors busy. The Northwest is a popular locale among producers of car commercials, mainly for its wooded, winding, rainy roads and for consumer products being marketed for their "natural and wholesome" qualities.

## *Casting*

Seattle has a small minority population, and this is reflected in its casting. Not only are ethnic actors in low demand, but women have to struggle in the male-dominated field.

Fringe theater offers the most possibilities for ethnic and minority actors. There are a few constituent-specific theater companies such as The Alice B. Theater for women, the Northwest Asian-American Theater, and the Taproot Theater Company (Christian). The Group Theater is considered multicultural.

Most of the industrial work goes to corporate-looking types, both men and women who can be spokespeople for the company. For commercials, the most prevalent look is the outdoorsy WASP type—the kind of people who eat granola and drive BMWs.

## Networking

The Capitol Hill area is where the main fringe theaters are located, and the restaurants near Broadway are favorite stopping sites. But the principle networking location is at The Play's the Thing. This bookstore has an upstairs lounge where people gather and a downstairs area that is available for informal readings. The New York, LA, and San Francisco trade publications are available at the bookstore, and a bulletin board contains audition notices and announcements.

*The Play's the Thing*
    ADDRESS: Drama Bookstore, 514 E. Pike, Seattle, WA 98104
    PHONE: (206) 322-7529

## Talent Agents and Casting Directors

Agents sign actors on an exclusive basis, with the union agents considered to be the top of the field. Competition for agents has grown stronger in the past few years, but stage actors can deal exclusively with the theaters rather than going through agents or casting directors.

Most film and commercial actors have agents, but they can also submit their P&R directly to casting directors. Many of the casting directors work directly with the actors, skipping the agents.

## Talent Unions

*Actor's Equity Association* (Equity), Liaison City
    MEMBERS: 400
    ADDRESS/PHONE: see the section on talent unions under Los Angeles

*American Federation of Television and Radio Artists* (AFTRA)
    MEMBERS: 1,000
    ADDRESS: 601 Valley St., #100, Seattle, WA 98109
    PHONE: (206) 282-2506

*Screen Actors' Guild (SAG)*
ADDRESS/PHONE: same as AFTRA

## **Professional Associations**

*League of Fringe Theaters (LOFT)*
ADDRESS: 1710 37th Ave., Seattle, WA 98122
PHONE: (206) 328-4321
. This not-for-profit corporation produces the Annual Seattle Fringe Theater Festival and LOFT general auditions. Members receive priority at the auditions, a monthly newsletter, hotline access, and discounts on workshops.

*New City Theater*
ADDRESS: 1634 11th Ave., Seattle, WA 98122
PHONE: (206) 323-6801
This fringe theater produces a Playwrights' Festival every fall and a Directors' Festival every spring. General auditions are held twice a year.

*Northwest Playwrights Guild*
ADDRESS: P.O. Box 95259, Seattle, WA 98145
PHONE: (206) 365-6026
The Northwest Playwrights Guild's reading series and festivals use actor volunteers in conjunction with theater companies in both Seattle and Portland. Actors interested in participating can send their P&R to the above address.

## **Publications**

*The Actor's Handbook*
(Seattle; Capitol Hill Press, Inc. 1991)
This handbook, edited by Ellen Taft, was written by local actors and is a valuable source for anyone trying to work in the area. Supplements are published periodically and are available at The Play's the Thing in Seattle and Powell's in Portland.

*The Northwest Film, Video and Audio Production Index*
. ADDRESS: P.O. Box 24365, Seattle, WA 98124

*Seattle Post-Intelligencer*
This newspaper posts audition notices in their Friday edition in the audition column.

*Seattle Weekly*
This paper is published weekly and posts audition notices in the *Callboard* column.

## *Talent Books*

*Contact Seattle* (LOFT)
ADDRESS: 1710 37th Ave., Seattle, WA 98122
PHONE: (206) 323-4321
This organization maintains a P&R file that is available to theaters and producers. Your P&R can be included in different categories.

## *Talent Showcases*

*Northwest Drama Conference*
ADDRESS: University of Alaska at Anchorage, 3211 Providence Dr., Anchorage, AL 99508
This annual combined audition is held in February in different Northwest locations. It is primarily for students and non-Equity actors.

*Regional Equity Actors* (REACT)
ADDRESS/PHONE: see the talent unions section above
Regional Equity sponsors local auditions for regional theaters across the country. Participating actors pay a low fee to cover the cost of bringing casting directors to Seattle.

*League of Fringe Theaters*
ADDRESS/PHONE: see the professional associations section above
The League has two auditions a year that are announced on the LOFT hotline.

## Miami and South Florida

Like the Northwest, the Southern states get more than their fair share of actors escaping the harsh realities of winter and the frenetic pace of the bigger cities for long white beaches and warm, sunny skies. However the difficulty in working in the South is that a lot of good employment is spread between rather distant towns.

Miami in itself extends for nearly fifty miles along the southern coast of Florida, and it is four hours away from Orlando, with its numerous production stages at Universal Studios and Disney Studios Florida. But many actors live in Miami and commute to wherever the work can be found—even to New York in the summer or LA during the pilot season.

Things change quickly in Miami, and it's difficult to say what type of performance art will boom next. When *Miami Vice* was in production, many local actors got their break in television. Recently, the theater seems to be getting all of the attention.

If you happen to be a theater actor or interested in doing commercials in the South, then Miami is the place to be. If you want to act in television or film, then Orlando has become the hot locale. Beepers are big in Miami, for the purpose of keeping your exact location vague when casting directors call.

*Training*

Many of the local theaters have an affiliated school or training program, such as the Burt Reynolds Institute for Theater Training (BRITT) whose students get small parts on the stage of the Tecquestah Theater. The Professional Actors Association of Florida holds Monday night workshops that are open to members (non-members are by audition). These workshops are a great way to work on your skills and network at the same time. However, most professional actors tend to go to New York to get additional training.

*Certificate and Degree Programs*

*University of Miami*, Department of Theater Arts

ADDRESS: P.O. Box 248273, Coral Gables, FL 33124
PHONE: (305) 284-6439

### Theater

There are theaters and companies all over the South, from Miami to Jacksonville, from Atlanta to Tallahassee. But the majority of theater takes place in Fort Lauderdale/Miami up to West Palm Beach.

The largest presenting houses are partially state-funded LORT theaters such as the Caldwell Theater Company and the Coconut Grove Playhouse. Unfortunately, these productions are primarily cast in New York.

Some Equity theaters, such as the Actor's Playhouse and The Public Theater of Greater Fort Lauderdale, operate under SPT agreements, while others, such as the Acme Acting Company and the Ann White Theater, use LOA and Guest Artist contracts. These theaters tend to stage traditional dramas and musicals that cater to the retirement crowd.

Equity theaters hold annual general auditions as well as per-show auditions which are announced on the union's hotline. The Florida Professional Theaters Association general auditions are attended by Equity and non-Equity theaters from all over the state.

Non-union theaters include the New Theater, the Red Barn Theater, and the Teatro Avante. These theaters tend to produce the more experimental works in Florida. You can use the newspapers to find out about casting as well as theater listings.

Dinner theaters seem to appeal to retirees in Florida because it's an easy way for the older crowd to get a full night's entertainment—drinks, dinner, and a show—without having to drive around. These productions tend to be strictly traditional, and theaters such as Theater Club of Palm Beaches, the Jupiter Theater, and the Royal Palm keep a large pool of actors working. There is also a large Latino community in South Florida that supports all-Spanish productions.

## Film and Television

Despite Florida being a right-to-work state, the unions are strong. Five years of *Miami Vice* gave quite a few local actors their SAG cards (Florida has the third largest branch in the country).

There are also quite a few television series which make their home in Orlando at the ever-expanding sound stages of Universal and MGM. Though many of the features and series are cast in New York and LA, the sheer quantity of these productions means there are day player, extra, and under-five work for local actors.

Make sure you have a good agent or strong ties with casting companies in Orlando, even if you don't live there. Miami agents get called only when there's trouble casting a role, despite the fact that the largest pool of actors live in Miami.

## Industrials and Commercials

Though corporate production is increasing in South Florida, relatively few actors make a living doing union and non-union industrials. There are, however, a fair amount of trade and industrial shows that need live performers for spokesmen and women. Many cruise lines cast from Miami for their stage shows. Agents rather than casting directors usually get you the work.

Commercials, on the other hand, can provide a nice living, especially in the winter months. Miami is a popular location spot, with its palm trees, beaches, and art deco buildings. Locals are regularly cast as principals, and you can send your P&R directly to production houses and advertising agencies.

## Casting

Commercials are looking for actors with natural beauty and a slim athletic body since a lot of work is done around water with the actors in skimpy summer clothing. When it comes to industrials, companies mainly seek actors with a corporate look to serve as spokesmen and women.

There's also a huge Spanish-speaking community, generating work for actors on local networks, dramas, and commercials. The acting pool is tightly knit and resents the influx of Northern talent and bilingual actors will find they must heavily network their way into meeting production staff and casting directors.

Constituency-specific theaters include the non-Equity Teatro Avante which produces plays both in Spanish and in English and the Vinnete Carroll Theater which focuses on drama for and about people of color.

### Networking

It's difficult to network when everything is so spread out. There's also no trade paper to hold the community together. The best way to meet other actors is to attend AFTRA and SAG activities, as well as those held by other professional organizations in the area.

### Talent Agents and Casting Directors

The majority of agents and casting directors are located in Miami, but more are relocating to Orlando to be near the big production studios. The unions can provide a list of franchised agents, and it isn't difficult to get an appointment. In Florida, like anywhere else, it's up to the actor to keep his or her name and face in the agent's mind, and to call regularly to find out about audition possibilities.

You won't find many exclusive contracts in the South, perhaps because the work bounces around. Yet for every rule there is an exception. The Talent Network, for instance, likes to work with exclusive talent. Most actors list with several agents.

Casting directors do call actors directly, but even then agents are brought in to negotiate the contract. For work in the theater, unlike in film and television, actors can get by without an agent simply by making good contacts with the local theaters.

### Talent Unions

*Actors' Equity Association* (Equity), Liaison City
MEMBERS: 500 (South Florida)

*American Federation of Television Radio Artists* (AFTRA)
MEMBERS: 700 (Miami)
ADDRESS: 20401 N.W. 2nd Ave, #102, Miami, FL 33169
PHONE: (305) 652-4842

*Screen Actors' Guild* (SAG)
MEMBERS: 3,000 (Florida)
ADDRESS: 2299 Douglas Rd., #200, Miami, FL 33145
PHONE: (305) 444-7677

### Professional Associations

*Florida Professional Theaters Association* (FPTA)
ADDRESS: P.O. Box 3805, West Palm Beach, FL 33402
PHONE: (407) 848-6231
This organization is for theaters and individuals. Services include a bimonthly newsletter, the quarterly publication *Callboard*, workshops, and a P&R file.

*Professional Actors Association of Florida* (PAAF)
ADDRESS: P.O. Box 610366, Miami Beach, FL 33161
PHONE: (305) 932-1427
This not-for-profit organization provides support and services for the acting community, including workshops, a talent directory, and outreach to production personnel. Membership requirements are tough: two years with the union and at least three principal speaking parts under union contracts within the previous two years. However, nonmembers can participate in workshops and showcases by audition.

### Publications

*Florida Professional Theaters Association Callboard*
ADDRESS/PHONE: see the professional organizations section above
This quarterly publication is included with membership dues. It provides audition notices and other information relevant to the acting community.

## Talent Books

*American Federation of Television and Radio Artists*
ADDRESS/PHONE: see the talent unions section above
The union office keeps members' P&Rs and voice-over tapes on file.

*Florida Professional Theaters Association*
ADRESS/PHONE: see the professional organizations section above
Members' P&Rs are kept in the FPTA talent file.

*PAAF*
ADDRESS/PHONE: see the professional organizations section above
PAAF sends its directory of members to producers, casting personnel, and directors across the country.

## Talent Showcases

*Florida Professional Theaters Association* (FPTA)
ADDRESS/PHONE: see the professional organizations section above
This organization holds annual auditions in late summer or early fall that are attended by member theaters and commercial and corporate film producers. Non-Equity actors must be FPTA members, while Equity members may audition but are encouraged to join FPTA.

*PAAF*
ADDRESS/PHONE: see the professional organizations section above
This organization presents an annual showcase of scenes, monologues, and songs. Members and nonmembers may audition at the monthly workshops, and an annual open call is announced on the Equity hotline and in the local newspapers the *Sun-Sentinel* and the *Miami Herald*.

*Southeastern Theater Conference*, University of North Carolina

ADDRESS: 506 Stirling St., Greensboro, NC 27412

PHONE: (919) 272-3645

This showcase is held annually in September in Atlanta, Georgia, and in March in various cities in the South. Experienced Equity and non-Equity actors may audition, but Equity theaters can only hire non-Equity actors for apprentice positions.

## Dallas

Dallas is the media center for Texas and the surrounding states and it has one of the highest rates of film production in the nation. So if you want to work in TV and film, yet you don't want to fight the competition in LA or pay the prices in New York, Dallas could be the place for you.

A theater actor may have to commute between Dallas, Houston, and Austin to find enough stage work. Houston also has some film productions, due to its locale, while San Antonio is gaining in the film and broadcast markets.

Texas, like Florida, is a right-to-work state, so non-union talent can work without having to join the union. This has a discernable affect on local unions, which are supported less in this state than anywhere else in this book. In fact, many experienced actors refrain from joining the union until they are ready to leave for New York or LA and want to have their card in hand before arriving in those cities.

Casting personnel in Texas aren't overly impressed by East and West coast credentials. There's a lot of local hiring, especially of actors who worked in the larger cities but have returned to Dallas.

### *Training*

Most of the local training is for inexperienced actors although there are a few opportunities for advanced study with good coaches. The Society for Theatrical Artists' Guidance and Enchancement (STAGE) provides inexpensive workshops on technique, movement, and on-camera skills. And many local actors recommend the KD Studio, an accredited institution which offers a diploma in acting performance or an associates degree in Applied Arts.

*Certificate and Degree Programs*

*KD Studio*
ADDRESS: 2600 Stemmons Freeway, #117, Dallas, TX 75207
PHONE: (214) 638-0484

*University of Dallas*, Drama Department
ADDRESS: 1845 E. Northgate Dr., Irving, TX 75062
PHONE: (214) 721-5061

*University of Texas at Dallas*
ADDRESS: P.O. Box 830688, Richardson, TX 75083
PHONE: (214) 690-2341

## *Theater*

There are at least fifty theaters in the Dallas/Fort Worth area—mostly smaller, nonunion stages. Dallas has always been known for its Theater in the Round, one of the first regional theaters in the country.

Among the established Equity theaters are the Dallas Theater Center and Theater Three. Others, such as Addison Center Theater, Casa Manana, Open Stage, and Stage West, are a mixture of non-union and affiliated productions using SPT, Guest Artist contracts, or LOAs. These companies tend to produce shows that will appeal to the older theater-going community like traditional Broadway musicals and plays.

The more non-traditional and progressive productions are left to the smaller, nonunion companies. These are occasionally produced under the Equity Members Project Code.

Most auditions are announced in *Centerstage* or on the STAGE bulletin board. It's not too difficult to get audition spots and monologues are requested.

## Film and Television

Texas is a popular location site for film and television productions; Oliver Stone seems to love filming in the area. Locals get lots of work when films come south, though the principal and secondary roles are usually cast before they arrive. There is always a need for day players, under-fives, and extras.

The television show *Dallas* was wonderful for the acting community. It was on the air for thirteen years, and half of the shows were shot locally. Other successful series have been produced in this area, including *Texas Ranger* and *Walker*.

## Industrials and Commercials

Many major corporations moved to Texas during the boom of the '80s and corporate work is still going strong. There is a mixture of union and non-union productions, yet SAG talent is sought after and these actors can usually perform under limited agreements.

The commercial market accounts for almost three-fourths of the work going through the AFTRA/SAG office. Production is done primarily by advertising agencies and in-house production teams.

## Casting

Texas is rather conservative, and casts accordingly. Character types don't do as well as the clean-cut, All-American type. Think football and cowboys (with the attendant female equivalents) and you've got the picture.

The Spanish-language community is large, and Latino actors can find plenty of work in local commercials, networks, and in constituent-specific theaters such as Teatro Dallas. The Callier Theater of the Deaf utilizes both auditory and hearing-impaired actors and two of the local black companies are the Jubilee Theater and the Vivid Theater Ensemble. There's also a lot of voice-over work in the South, though again it's male-dominated.

## Networking

Undoubtedly, the most productive networking can be done through STAGE events.

Though the community is spread across a large area, there are some pockets where actors tend to congregate; lower Greenville has a few bars near the small theater companies and Deep Ellum, at the east end of downtown Dallas, is also popular.

### Talent Agents and Casting Directors

In Texas actors must work on an exclusive, signed basis with agents. Most actors find they need an agent, particularly those in film and broadcasting. The unions can provide a list of franchised agents; even if you are a non-union actor it can be beneficial to use with a union agent.

Local casting directors are accessible and you can send them your P&R and call for an appointment. You can also check the *Dallas Actors' Handbook* to find production companies and corporations who keep in-house casting files.

### Talent Unions

*Actors' Equity Association* (Equity), Liaison City
MEMBERS: 400 (Dallas/Fort Worth)

*American Federation of Television and Radio Artists* (AFTRA)
MEMBERS: 600
ADDRESS: 6060 North Central Expressway, #302, LB 604, Dallas, TX 75206
PHONE: (214) 363-8300

*Screen Actors' Guild* (SAG)
MEMBERS: 600
ADDRESS/PHONE: same as AFTRA

### Professional Associations

*The Society for Theatrical Artists' Guidance and Enhancement* (STAGE)

ADDRESS: 4633 Insurance Lane, Dallas, TX 75221
PHONE: (214) 559-3917

This not-for-profit organization offers numerous services to actors, including talent showcases, bulletin board, a casting file, newsletter, classes, and group health insurance.

## *Publications*

*Centerstage*
ADDRESS/PHONE: see the professional association section above

This monthly publication is sent to STAGE members and includes news, announcements, audition notices, articles, and a list of area theaters.

*Dallas Actors' Handbook* by Dale Kassel
(Irving, Texas: Handbook Publications)

This booklet is updated every year and provides lists of talent agents, casting companies, theaters, corporate producers, production houses, and advertising agencies, along with who accepts P&Rs. It also provides resource lists of coaches, photographers, and services.

*Dallas Observer*
This free weekly publication has a few non-union audition notices.

## *Talent Books*

The *Official Southwest Talent Directory*
ADDRESS: 2908 McKinney Ave., Dallas, TX 75221
PHONE: (214) 754-4729

This directory is distributed to agents and casting directors. You must have an agent or be a union member to be included.

*Society for Theatrical Artists' Guidance and Enhancement*
ADDRESS/PHONE: see the professional associations section above

Members can keep their P&R on file at the STAGE office. Local casting personnel and directors frequently use this listing.

## Talent Showcases

*Southwest Theater Association*, Lubbock Christian University
ADDRESS: 5601 19th St., Lubbock, TX 79407

This talent showcase is held every year in late February in Lubbock, Texas. Both Equity and non-Equity actors may participate.

*Society for Theatrical Artists' Guidance and Enhancement*
ADDRESS/PHONE: see the professional associations section above

The Society sponsors six scene showcases each year in which five two-person scenes are presented to agents, producers, and casting directors. All STAGE members may audition and are judged by a panel of casting directors. Each summer, STAGE also produces a festival of four previously unproduced plays. Auditions are announced in *Centerstage*.

# 8 | *Surviving as an Actor*

Actors don't have it easy. Beginning actors have to train for years and usually have to work without pay in order to be seen by casting directors and agents. And even if you land a job, it only lasts a limited time. After what amounts to weeks or months of auditioning, actors are often lucky to end up with one day's work on a commercial or a few days on a soap or sitcom.

Most actors need to have a survival job in order to support themselves between acting roles. Sure, you can save money to live on so you can focus entirely on your acting career, but that can't last forever unless you have a trust fund or overindulgent parents. Even if you are getting acting jobs, the work won't be steady until you've established yourself. And that takes years.

If you rely on acting to survive then you'll start to get desperate for work. Nothing can ruin an actor's career quicker than desperation. Casting personnel can tell when you are dying for a role, and that panic will come through instead of the character.

You have to consider the best way to support yourself while you're pursuing your acting career. There are lots of different jobs that are compatible with an actor's lifestyle. You need work that is flexible enough for you to attend auditions, interviews, and classes. You also need a job that can easily be set aside during those periods when you *have* landed a role.

The following list of job possibilities are wide ranging, and it's up to you to find a survival job that is both satisfying and challenging. If you don't, you'll feel beaten down by the daily grind of earning your living and you won't be able to give any energy to your acting.

## Survival Jobs

### *Related Acting Work*

There are a number of related jobs in the acting industry, and many actors naturally turn to this field when they aren't working. Teaching is such a popular way for out-of-work actors to make a living that beginning actors must be careful who they go to for lessons. Established, career actors however, can make a respectable living teaching others the craft.

Modeling is such a closely related field that it's worth it for every actor to pursue job opportunities, whether it's in hand modeling or catalog work. Modeling is a great way to make a lot of money in a relatively few hours. And the process of auditioning for jobs is compatible with an actor's lifestyle.

Productions always hire short-term help, whether it's for a stage, studio, or location shoot. Every aspect of production offers an actor opportunities to work: production assistant, lighting, set building, wardrobe, make-up, hairstyling, not to mention low-paying jobs such as ushering and taking tickets.

By using whatever skills you have in the acting industry, you'll increase your networking possibilities. Many actors shy away from this, believing that a "serious" artist wouldn't be seen performing more menial work. But every minute you're in the presence of professionals you'll be hearing the behind-the-scenes scoop on what directors like and want and what other working actors are doing to get the parts.

Your goal is to get into the acting industry, so why not do it any way you can? Once you have your foot in the door, you'll start meeting people and finding out about upcoming projects as well as who to contact in order to be seen and remembered.

## *Office Work*

Temp work has become the actor's mecca of the 21st century. With a set of business clothes and computer skills that are easily learned with a few hours of classes, even an actor can pass as a respectable 9–5 employee. The best thing about temping is that it's flexible on a day to day basis—perfect for last-minute auditions. You can work any hours or any shift you're available for by simply putting yourself on call at a temp agency. In the larger cities, law offices regularly hire temps to work evenings and night shifts. Day rates are approximately $12–$18 an hour, while night work can be $25 an hour or more.

An administrative assistant combines secretarial work with office administration, often setting up appointments and assisting a senior executive, as well as delegating the clerking and receptionist duties. Depending on the size of the company, a good administrative assistant can work flexible hours and days, and charge approximately $10–$25 an hour depending on his or her experience.

A personal assistant usually combines light secretarial work with errand-running—from picking up dry cleaning to organizing a cocktail party. The flexibility of your hours depends on your boss, but personal assistants can make $15–$20 an hour.

Telemarketers work for companies that are trying to sell their product over the phone. You have to memorize a spiel and give it convincingly enough to hook the customer (think of it as an acting challenge). The hourly pay is low, but if you're good at phone work, you can find jobs that will pay a commission on each sale.

## *Tip Work*

Waiting tables and acting seem to go hand in hand, especially in New York where it seems like almost everyone who takes your order is secretly aspiring to be the next Broadway sensation. Waiters can work either in restaurants or for caterers. Caterers seem to make it a practice to hire actors, and why not? They get attractive, groomed employees who are willing to work for only a few hours a day. Restaurants can be more wary of hiring actors because the attrition level is high due to missed work. (Who can ever forget that classic scene from *A Chorus Line* where a dancer babbles on about how he's going to lose his job as a waiter because the audition has made him late again?)

Hotels often hire part-time bellhops to work weekend shifts or for extra help during peak hours around check-out time. Depending on the quality of the hotel, a bellhop can make $50–$150 a day.

Coat check attendants can make $1 a coat in tips, and depending on the size of the establishment, tips can range from $50–$150 a night. When coat check attendants work for caterers on a flexible basis, they usually make $10 an hour and aren't allowed to solicit tips.

### Service Jobs

Being a hairstylist is a creative way for actors to make ends meet and it is a great job when it comes to flexibility. You can work at home or in a salon (with a state license) or travel to your client's homes. You can schedule your appointments around your acting, and even if you have to cancel because of a last-minute audition, your steady clientele will usually understand after spending hours talking to you while their hair is being cut. With tips, hairstylists can make $10–$30 an hour.

Tutoring high school or college students is a great way to earn a high hourly wage, whether the subject is math, creative writing, or foreign languages. Tutors can work through an agency or advertise directly on bulletin boards at campus. You can even tutor or teach music to grade-school children.

If you love animals, then there are plenty of part-time opportunities in almost every aspect of the pet industry. It only takes a few months to learn the basics of dog grooming or dog training, and then you can set up your own business. Groomers and trainers charge anywhere from $10–$30 an hour for their services.

Massage therapy is a rewarding job, but it takes serious training and time to build up a steady clientele. Usually it helps to be associated with a reputable institute or a four-star hotel. The hourly rate is very high: $40–$100 an hour.

Yard work, such as gardening, maintaining lawns, playgrounds, or cleaning pools can be good work in the warmer climates where winter won't put a halt to your income. The pay is low, $8–$15 an hour, but the work is physically satisfying and mentally undemanding.

### Skilled Labor

If you have a skill in electronics or computers, you can sell your expertise as a consultant or repairman. Computer consultants must be knowledgeable about current hardware and software in order to teach their clients how to set up and use their systems. Electronics repair work can include anything from VCRs and televisions to car stereos.

Construction is also a great way to make good money. Carpenters are often self-employed and advertise in the yellow pages and local papers for small construction jobs, anything from building a set of shelves to an outside deck. Any sort of short-term carpentry work usually costs $20 an hour.

You can also do specialty work through supply companies. Carpet stores often hire freelancers to install carpets for their customers. Housepainters, tile-layers, and plasterers can also work through a hardware stores or construction companies.

## Emotional Survival

An actor needs a support system of family, friends, and fellow actors in order to survive. If you don't have people you respect who you can talk to when you're feeling down, then you'll find it very hard to get out there and try again.

In order to maintain perspective, it's important to have a life outside of acting. Make sure you have other interests, or else you can start to place too much importance on your status within the narrow world of acting. Do something else creative, like playing an instrument or taking an art class. And maintain your friendships outside of acting.

Many actors turn to this business because it satisfies their emotional needs—the desire for attention or respect from others, or as a way to express themselves. These can be powerful drives that you can harness in becoming an actor; yet if you don't have the emotional detachment to treat your career as a business, you'll never get past the naysayers. Even worse is the wall of silence that usually greets your best efforts. Actors must audition day after day in a never-ending process of looking for work, and if you can't control your reaction to the anxiety and the coldness of the business, then you won't be able to approach each audition afresh.

You need to have a healthy emotional life in order to trust your intuition. And you'll need every one of your inner resources in order to develop your talent and technique. By being aware of your own feelings, by acknowledging each disappointment, you can clear everything away to make room for the next experience.

The only way to be a working actor is to learn how to enjoy the process of studying a character and auditioning. If you can be yourself and make the role your own, you'll have a better chance of impressing the casting people and directors.

Always try to think of acting as a business. You can't stake your self worth on every audition. Even if you were selling cars, you would feel bad when a potential customer bought a car from another dealer. It's even harder to detach yourself when the product you are selling is you. But rejection is not a reflection of you as a person, or even of you as an actor. It simply means that the role called for a different sort of character.

The best thing about the acting business is that the longer you're in it, the better are your chances of getting work. Many mature actors find they are given jobs based on past work that was seen and admired. But don't expect that someday you'll reach a level where you don't have to worry about getting jobs anymore. The reality is that you always have to make it happen for yourself; every role and every project. But if you love acting and you are willing to work at it, then you can making acting your life.

In an acting career, the rewards are like no other job—you have the freedom to express your talent and gain recognition, praise, and monetary returns. Working actors must learn to take pride in the creative process itself, in participating in the world of theater and entertainment, and in mastering their craft. For those who truly love to act, performing is the goal.

All it takes is to be a working actor is for you to launch your career as a business and persist until a pattern of work develops. Working actors are not necessarily more talented than those who quit and change careers. They simply have more tenacity and an unquenchable determination to succeed. They are also realistic about their probable rate of.success and they don't expect miracles to happen overnight. But if you want to act, then you can have a creative, challenging career, worth every effort you make.

# *Index*